Fast Python: Master the Basics to Write Faster Code

Chris Conlan

Contents

5 Declaring Things 121

6 Miscellaneous Topics 135

Fast Python: Master the Basics to Write Faster Code
Chris Conlan
Bethesda, Maryland
USA

ISBN-13: 979-8-6327-8498-6

About the Author
Chris Conlan is the founder and CEO of Conlan Scientific, a financial data science consultancy based out of Bethesda, Maryland. He works with his team of data scientists to build machine learning solutions for banks, lenders, investors, traders, and fintech companies. Chris graduated University of Virginia's College of Arts & Sciences with a degree in statistics, where he later co-taught a data science capstone course.

About the Technical Reviewer
Will Angel is the author of Virtual Power, an organizer for the Data Visualization DC meetup group, and a board member for Data Community DC, a non-profit educational organization.

Chapter 1

Introduction

The Python programming language has a large and active community. As a result, there is a lot of a material online about various ways to speed up your code. When programmers try to optimize the execution speed of a given algorithm, they will typically study multiple variants of it with code profiling tools. *Code profiling* involves empirically studying the behavior of an algorithm, typically with the goal of reducing its execution time.

In college, most computer science majors will take something resembling Algorithms 101, where they discuss the language-agnostic principles of execution time in terms of computational complexity. The *computational complexity* of an algorithm can be analyzed and derived on paper, independent of any specific programming language. Discussions about computational complexity typically look like mathematical proofs.

This book attempts to integrate lessons from code profiling and computational complexity to help readers master the basics of Python and write faster code. By studying the basics in this way, we will end up revealing many fundamental principles of code optimization. After reading this book, readers should be able to consistently apply these lessons to their own code. Additionally, they should have more confidence that their own first-draft algorithms are optimal, and they will have the necessary tools and knowledge to make improvements to them.

In the process of exploring these algorithms, we will make some novel discoveries and disprove some myths about the Python language. For each algorithm, we will iteratively hyper-optimize its performance using a wide variety of Python libraries. Each discussion will end with a series of tables and charts from the code profiles of these algorithms.

The rest of this chapter will discuss prerequisite knowledge for following along with this book. Feel free to skip ahead to Chapter 2 if you are familiar with these topics.

1.1   Libraries

We will make heavy use of `pandas`, `numpy`, `matplotlib`, `numba`, and `typing` throughout this book. Code samples will appear with the assumption that readers have imported the following in the following way.

```python
import numpy as np
import pandas as pd
from numba import jit
import matplotlib.pyplot as plt
from typing import Dict, List, Tuple, Any, NewType
```

1.2   Type Hints

Python is a dynamically typed language, which is good for development speed, but bad for readability. I prefer to use type hints when possible to improve readability.

In Python 3.5, the `typing` module was added to the standard library, as well as syntactical support for type hints. A lot of custom Python compilers and IDE's have been released that try to *do* something with these type hints, but standard compilers basically ignore them. They mostly exist for the benefit of developers and future readers of their code.

Type hints primarily help developers write and handle complex data types. For example, I can document the following complex data types.

```python
from typing import List, Dict, Tuple, Any
import datetime

# A list of floating point numbers
v: List[float] = [i * 1.23 for i in range(10)]

# A list of mixed type values
v: List[Any] = ['apple', 123, 'banana', None]

# A dictionary of floats indexed by dates
v: Dict[datetime.date, float] = {
    datetime.date.today(): 123.456,
    datetime.date(2000, 1, 1): 234.567,
}

# A dictionary of lists of strings indexed by tuples of
# integers
v: Dict[Tuple[int, int], List[str]] = {
    (2, 3): [
        'apple',
        'banana',
    ],
    (4, 7): [
        'orange',
        'pineapple',
    ]
}

# An incorrect type hint
# Your compiler or IDE might complain about this
v: List[str] = [1, 2, 3]

# A possibly incorrect type hint
# There is no concensus on whether or not this is correct
v: List[float] = [1, None, 3, None, 5]

# This is non-descript but correct
v: List = [(1,2,'a'), (4,5,'b')]

# This is more descriptive
v: List[Tuple[int, int, str]] = [(1,2,'a'), (4,5,'b')]
```

```python
# Custom types are supported
from typing import NewType
FruitType = NewType('FruitType', str)
fruit_type: FruitType = 'APPLE'

# Functions can define input and return types
def convert_to_string(value: Any) -> str:
    return str(value)
```

Listing 1.1: Type-hinting examples

1.3 Computational Complexity

Throughout this book, we will speak casually about the computational complexity of algorithms. When we use the word *complexity*, unqualified, we are speaking about *time complexity*, which describes the relationship between the runtime of an algorithm and the dimensions of its inputs.

We will discuss computational complexity in terms of Big-O notation. We will make statements like, "this algorithm runs in $\mathcal{O}(n^2)$ time," or, "this algorithm is $\mathcal{O}(nm)$." The Big-O has a mathematical definition that is independent of computer science. The definition can be simplified a little for computer science, because runtimes and dimensions are strictly positive. The formula is as follows.

If $f(x) = \mathcal{O}(g(x))$, then $f(x) \leq Mg(x)$ as $x \to \infty$ for some constant M.

The function $g(x)$ is essentially the growth behavior of $f(x)$. In our discussions, $f(x)$ represents the runtime of the algorithm, and $g(x)$ represents the growth behavior in terms of the dimensions of its parameters. In computer science, x, $f(x)$, and $g(x)$ are strictly positive. Occasionally, we might discuss other types of complexity, like memory complexity, using the same notation.

Readers can see this Wikipedia article, https://en.wikipedia.org/wiki/Big_O_notation, for a more rigorous mathematical explanation of Big-O notation if desired.

It is worth noting that basic principles of calculus and limit theorems apply to Big-O notation. For example, $f(x) = 3x^2 + 2x + 5 =$

$\mathcal{O}(x^2)$ because $f(x) \leq 4x^2$ as $x \to \infty$, where the number 4 is chosen arbitrarily because it is larger than 3. This will become important when we analyze algorithms. In other words, small jobs that happen before and after the core computations will end up having no effect on the Big-O value, because they behave similarly to the $2x$ or the 5 in the above equation.

One of the skills we will develop in this book is the ability to determine the Big-O value of an algorithm purely by observation of the code. In other words, readers should eventually be able to confidently determine the Big-O value of an algorithm without profiling it or running any tests on it. When we do this, we will typically look at the number of operations of some type occurring in the body of the algorithm. Operations we might count include basic arithmetic operations, comparison operations, and lookup operations. We will also have to rely on our computer science savvy to know which Python algorithms might incur hidden complexity. For example, a call to the **sum()** function in Python can have different implications for computational complexity based on the characteristics of its arguments.

See Listing 1.2 for some very basic examples of operations, along with their computational complexity.

```python
def add_two(x: float, y: float) -> float:
    """
    O(1) because is performs one addition
    """
    return x + y


def add_a_few(x: float, y: float, z: float) -> float:
    """
    O(1) because is performs 2 additions
    """
    return x + y + z


def loop_through_it(n: int) -> int:
    """
    O(n) because it performs n additions
    """
    value = 0
    for i in range(n):
        value += i
```

```python
    return value

def loop_through_it_squarely(n: int) -> int:
    """
    O(n^2) because it performs 2*n^2 additions
    """
    value = 0
    for i in range(n):
        for j in range(n):
            value += i + j
    return value

def loop_through_it_twice(n: int) -> int:
    """
    O(n) because it performs 2*n additions and n
    multiplications
    """
    value = 0
    for i in range(n):
        value += i
    for i in range(n):
        value += 2 * i
    return value
```

Listing 1.2: Computational complexity basics

See Table 1.1 for a list of common computational tasks and the computational complexity of their best-known algorithms.

Algorithm	Input dimensions	Complexity
Arithmetic operations	2	$\mathcal{O}(1)$
Sum of a vector of numbers	n	$\mathcal{O}(n)$
Sorting a list	n	$\mathcal{O}(n \log n)$
Lookup by index (list)	n	$\mathcal{O}(1)$
Finding an item (unsorted list)	n	$\mathcal{O}(n)$
Finding an item (sorted list)	n	$\mathcal{O}(\log n)$
Finding an item (hash table)	n	$\mathcal{O}(1)$
Matrix multiplication (square)	$2n^2$	$\mathcal{O}(n^{2.373})$
Matrix inversion	n^2	$\mathcal{O}(n^{2.373})$

Table 1.1: Complexity of best-known algorithms

Hopefully, this establishes the basics well enough that beginners will feel comfortable exploring the more complex (and useful) algorithms that will come along in this book. Alternatively, readers can ignore computational complexity altogether and solely rely on the compute-time charts littered throughout this book. In any case, you know what they say about teaching a man to fish.

1.4   Log-log Plots

Throughout this book, we will be studying the asymptotic behavior of algorithms per their input dimensions. The resulting differences in input dimensions and computation times will be exponentially different. For example, the compute time of an $\mathcal{O}(n)$ algorithm for an input size of 10,000 should be 1,000 times greater than the compute time for an input size of 10. Since our x and y values are both growing by exponential amounts, we will make heavy use of log-log plots.

Log-log plots are scaled logarithmically in both the x and y axes. Some of their properties are non-obvious, so we will discuss them here. The following mathematical argument is copied directly from the Wikipedia article on log-log plots that can be found here: https://en.wikipedia.org/wiki/Log-log_plot.

Given a monomial equation $y = ax^k$, taking the logarithm of the equation yields

$$\log y = k \log x + \log a.$$

Setting $x' = \log x$ and $y' = \log y$ yields the following familiar slope-intercept form for a line.

$$y' = mx' + b$$

for $m = k$ and $b = \log a$. This tells us that, on a log-log plot, monomial equations with the exponent k appear like lines with slope m. This will be important to remember as we explore and verify the computational complexity of various algorithms.

We can analyze the log-log appearance of any equation by writing the equation, taking the logarithm of both sides, and attempting to express it in terms of x' and y'. This is not always possible because logarithmic equations do not always have closed-form solutions. See Table 1.2 for some relevant results.

Base function	Log-log appearance
$y = 1/x$	$y' = -x'$
$y = \sqrt{x}$	$y' = x'/2$
$y = x$	$y' = x'$
$y = x^2$	$y' = 2x'$
$y = x^3$	$y' = 3x'$
$y = 5x^4$	$y' = 4x' + \log 5$
$y = e^x$	$y' = e^{x'}$
$y = \log x$	$y' = \log x'$
$y = x \log x$	$y' = x' + \log x'$
$y = x^2 \log x$	$y' = 2x' + \log x'$

Table 1.2: Common log-log functions

Keep in mind that, on a log-log plot, the visual distance between 10^{-10} and 1 is the same as the distance between 1 and 10^{10}, so we cannot truly observe the value of zero on a log-log plot without making false visual adjustments. Similarly, we cannot observe valid log-log plots with both positive and negative values on a single axis without making false visual adjustments. Some software supports this behavior, but we will disregard it and move on since all of our work will be strictly with values of x and y greater than zero.

Note that logarithmic functions and exponential functions appear the same on log-log plots as they do on normal Cartesian plots. Also note that monomials have a simple equation for log-log appearance but polynomials do not. For example, the polynomial $y = 3x^2 + 5x + 7$ cannot be expressed productively in terms of y' and x'. Nonetheless, it can be proven that the slope of y' approaches 2 as $x \to \infty$ because y is a degree-two polynomial. Similar results hold for degree-n polynomials. As mentioned previously, understanding of limit behaviors will be important for estimating the Big-O values of various algorithms.

See Figures 1.1 through 1.6 for examples of the above functions on log-log plots.

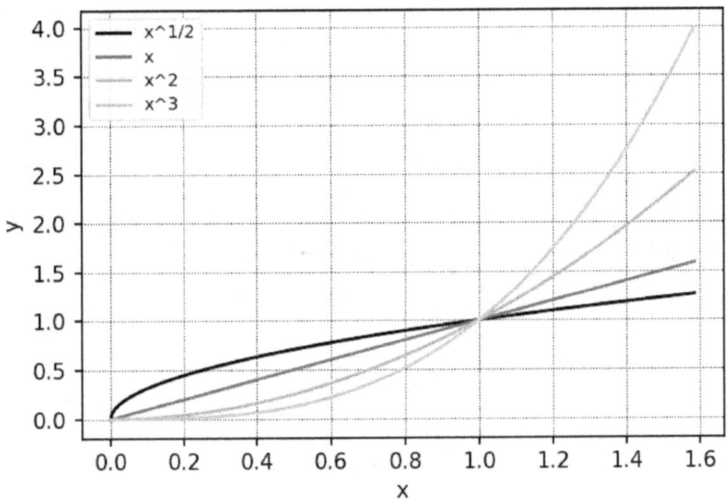

Figure 1.1: Vanilla monomials

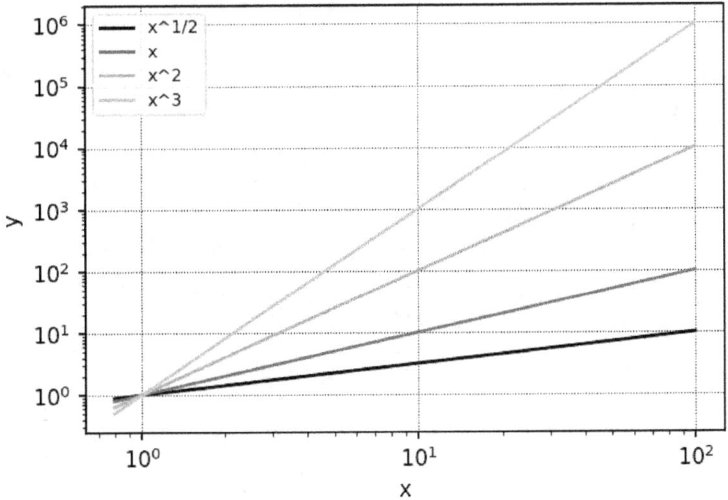

Figure 1.2: Log-log monomials

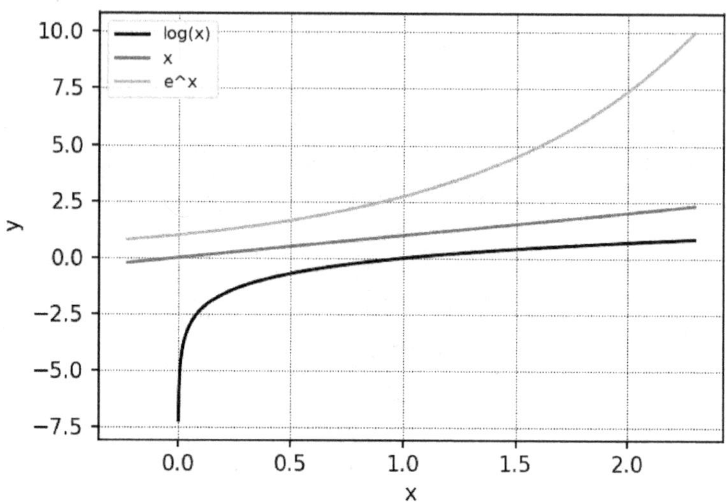

Figure 1.3: Vanilla exponentials

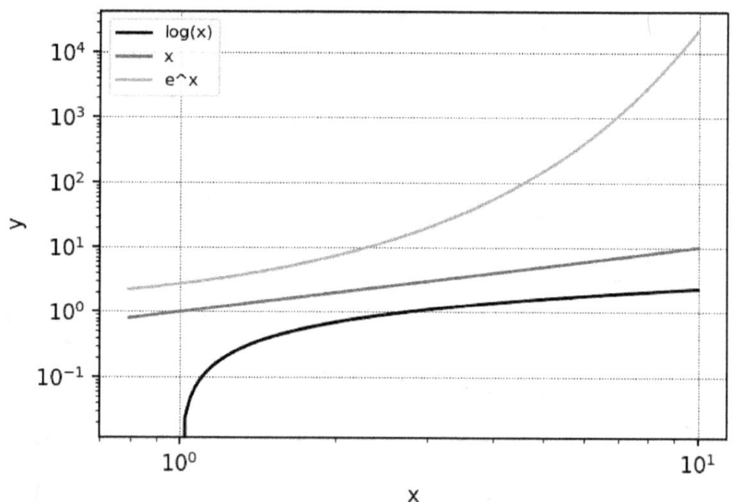

Figure 1.4: Log-log exponentials

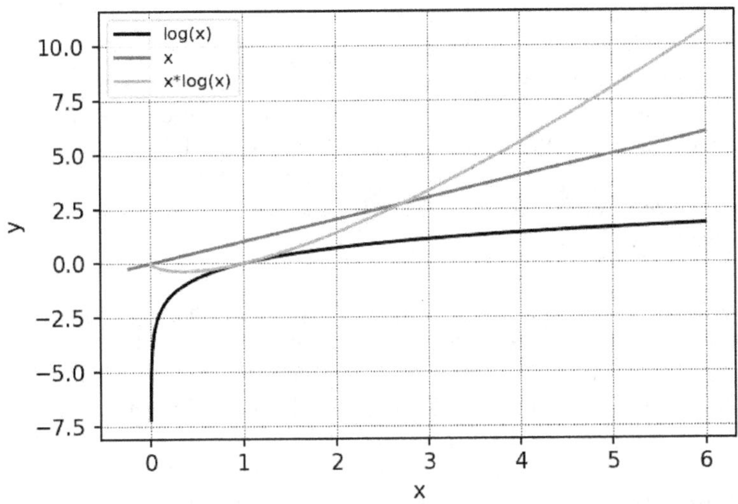

Figure 1.5: Vanilla compound functions

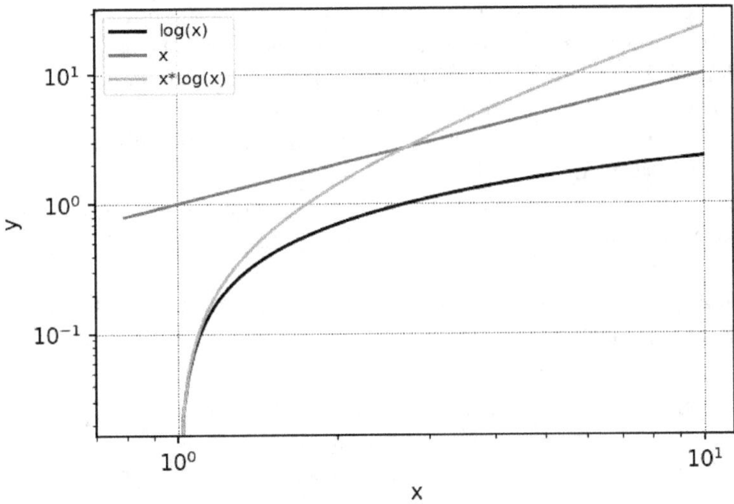

Figure 1.6: Log-log compound functions

1.5   Vectorization and Compilation

When optimizing algorithms, the first order of business is always to make sure it is running in the best possible time complexity. The next order of business to is to try to vectorize the calculation. In almost every chapter of this book, we will arrive at a point where we discover the best-known algorithm, then gain even more speed by vectorizing it.

Modern CPUs have instruction sets that are capable of processing multiple pieces of data within a single operation. These instruction sets are simply called vector instructions or *single instruction, multiple data* (SIMD) instruction sets. It is not important to fully understand what is happening at the hardware level in order to take advantage of this behavior. All you need to know is that carefully optimized compiled code can take advantage of this feature, and it can often provide order-of-magnitude improvements in execution time. Whether you know it or not, you have probably accessed and used such vectorized algorithms in the past via popular Python libraries.

This brings us to our next important point. Python is an interpreted programming language. This means that there is no compiler analyzing the code in an attempt to create efficiencies at the hardware level. Carefully written compiled code will generally be faster than the equivalent pure Python code for this reason. It is important to remember that utilizing vectorized algorithms in Python implies that we are taking advantage of carefully written compiled code.

Therefore, our progression from slow to fast in Python will typically follow this pattern.

1. Slow algorithm in pure Python.
2. Fast algorithm in pure Python.
3. Fast algorithm vectorized through Python library.

Some of the most interesting cases occur when the third step is impossible, or when the third step is impractical because the library requires too much overhead to offer a meaningful speed boost.

1.6   Github Repository and Updates

All of the code in this book is contained in a Github repository
here: https://github.com/chrisconlan/fast-python. The repo includes all of the code listings chapter-by-chapter, and all of the
scripts used to profile the functions.

Anyone is welcome to submit pull requests to the repository to
expand the library of both bad and good Python algorithms. I am
self-publishing this book, so I can issue new editions quickly if any
major additions are made. Because this book physically is small, I
have respected a line width limit of 60 throughout.

1.7   Tables and Plots

I use a small profiling module that was built specifically for this
book to profile, summarize, and chart the performance of the
functions we discuss. The output of each profile is a `pd.DataFrame`
detailing the performance of each run, and a series of log-log plots
comparing the performance of each function. Normally, these
charts are interactive `matplotlib` visualizations. When we profile
7 or 8 functions at once, they usually look like a funky diagonal
rainbow. In other words, they are pretty cool.

Due to the limitations of black and white printing, I have had to
pare down the charts a little. Since it is difficult to differentiate
between 4+ grayscale colors, I have opted to display a maximum
of 3 profiles at once in a chart. The 3 profiles I chose to display
were the fastest, slowest, and the median functions according to
their efficiency. Thus, for each set of functions we discuss, you will
see the following.

1. A table detailing the asymptotic behavior of all n functions
   we discussed.
2. A chart of execution time against input length for the 3 chosen functions.
3. A chart of efficiency against input length of for the 3 chosen
   functions.

Fortunately, readers can still render and explore the big colorful
`matplotlib` charts by downloading and running the scripts in the
GitHub repository. The profiler published in the Github repo is

configured for exploratory analysis, unlike the the version I am using, which is configured for typesetting black and white books.

1.8   Testing Environment

The results of the profiles in this book can vary based on the hardware and software supporting your testing environment. My testing environment is the computer I am writing this on, a 10-core Dell workstation running RedHat Linux 8. I am using Python 3.7 through an Anaconda environment, and all of the Python packages are installed through Anaconda's package manager.

While I am compelled to share the details of my own setup for scientific completeness, it is worth noting that the vast majority of algorithms we will profile in this book are not parallelized. In other words, users running anywhere between 2 and 99 CPU cores should see roughly the same performance as long as they do not encounter memory bottlenecks. If you do encounter memory bottlenecks while profiling, simply reduce the size of your input data so that it does not spill into swap memory.

You can run the profiles on your own computer using the code in the GitHub repo, and you should definitely do so if you suspect the results might differ on your own hardware and software.

1.9   Conclusion

Ultimately, the best way to learn about algorithms is by example. We will dive right into algorithms, complexity, and profiling in the next chapter.

Chapter 2

Adding Things

The content of this chapter was the inspiration for this book. We will work through all of the trivial and non-trivial ways you can add numbers, and hopefully learn something about speed.

2.1   Summing a List

For sake of completeness, we will discuss all the ways to sum a list of numbers. All of these algorithms will run in $\mathcal{O}(n)$ time for a list of numbers with length n, because I cannot think of any reasonable way to inefficiently sum a list of numbers. We will still manage to answer some relevant questions.

See Listings 2.1 and 2.2 for two pure Python implementations.

```python
def fast_sum(values: List[float]) -> float:
    accum = 0
    for value in values:
        accum += value
    return value
```

Listing 2.1: Fast sum in pure Python

There is a frequent misconception that natively implemented algorithms are always faster than those written out by hand. For example, programmers might think that Listing 2.1 must be slower than Listing 2.2, because the Python developers probably optimized the sum function in some way. This is not the case. The Python sum function implements virtually the same algorithm as Listing 2.1, in pure Python, under the hood. We can see from Table 2.1 that their performances are nearly identical.

```python
def fast_native_sum(values: List[float]) -> float:
    return sum(values)
```

Listing 2.2: Fast sum using Python's native sum

See Listings 2.3 and 2.4 for similar implementations in **numpy** and **pandas**. These functions are vectorized, so they will run much faster than pure Python functions.

```python
def numpy_fast_sum(values: np.ndarray) -> float:
    return np.sum(values)
```

Listing 2.3: Fast sum in numpy

Note that the input types to Listings 2.3 and 2.4 are **np.ndarray** and **pd.Series** respectively. These data structures are required to be present and initialized in order for the respective libraries to apply their vectorized algorithms. For example, if I had a list of numbers, I would have to wrap it with **np.array(my_list)** or **pd.Series(my_list)** before passing it to these functions. This step is not included in our calculation of the runtime, but it is important nonetheless.

```python
def pandas_fast_sum(values: pd.Series) -> float:
    return values.sum()
```

Listing 2.4: Fast sum in pandas

The **pandas** and **numpy** data structures typically have strict typing requirements that allow them to function with their compiled algorithms. For example, **numpy** needs to be sure that every single number in the **np.ndarray** is of the type **np.float64**, or a similar numeric type, in order to perform operations on them. The custom types utilized by **numpy** and **pandas** are deliberately more specific than those used in Python for this purpose.

The last summing function we will look at uses **numba** and will serve as a light introduction to **numba**. See Listing 2.5 for a summing implementation in **numba**.

The **jit** decorator from **numba** allows us to perform just-in-time (JIT) compilation of Python functions. We specify the `nopython=True` argument to the decorator to force **numba** to not use any Python code to connect the dots when doing JIT compilation. This limits what we are allowed to do in the function in some respects, but that is not a problem here.

Because the compilation occurs just-in-time rather than before the program is run, the compilation does not occur until the first time the function is actually used within the script. Therefore, for the purposes of profiling our code, we make sure to run a non-trivial computation at the module level before wrapping it in another caller.

Notice that the **_numba_fast_sum** definition looks exactly like the pure Python summing function in Listing 2.1, save for the type hint for the input argument. The **numba** library integrates closely with **numpy** and benefits from the strong typing supplied by **numpy**, so we will try to pass **np.ndarray** objects into **numba** functions whenever we can.

```python
from numba import jit
import numpy as np


@jit(nopython=True)
def _numba_fast_sum(values: np.ndarray) -> float:
    """
    JIT compilation occurs after one use
    """
    accum = 0
    for value in values:
        accum += value
    return accum


# Force numba to run jit compilation
_numba_fast_sum(np.random.random(100000))


def numba_fast_sum(values: np.ndarray) -> float:
    """
    Redeclare optimized wrapper
    """
    return _numba_fast_sum(values)
```

Listing 2.5: Fast sum with numba

See Table 2.1 for the compute-time results. As with many of the results in this book, it appears to be a close race between **numba** and **numpy** with **pandas** trailing slightly behind. Although **pandas** uses **numpy** for a lot of operations under the hood, it has some additional overhead that is responsible for much of its feature-rich API. We will discuss these features, and why they could potentially contribute to slowdowns, later in the book.

f	n	t (ms)	n/t
fast_sum	1E+08	9.6E+03	1.0E+04
fast_native_sum	1E+08	8.5E+03	1.2E+04
numpy_fast_sum	1E+08	6.6E+01	1.5E+06
pandas_fast_sum	1E+08	5.4E+02	1.9E+05
numba_fast_sum	1E+08	1.5E+02	6.7E+05

Table 2.1: Sum profiles

2.2   Calculating a Cumulative Sum

Calculating a cumulative sum is very similar to calculating a sum, except, instead of returning a single value, you return a list of numbers that represents the cumulative sum of the series. In other words, for a vector x_i for $i \in 1, ..., n$, the cumulative sum vector y_i is as follows.

$$y_i = \sum_{j=1}^{i} x_j$$

In the above equation, as well as in the algorithm, the output is a vector of the same length as the input vector.

This section will discuss the algorithm that served as the sole inspiration for this book. I have conducted a good number of programming tests over the years as part of job interviews, and I very frequently see the following incorrect variation of this algorithm. See Listing 2.6 for the infamously bad implementation of the cumulative sum algorithm.

```python
def slow_cusum(values: List[float]) -> List[float]:
    """
```

```python
    This is O(n^2) time, because it computes ...
    1
    1 + 2
    1 + 2 + 3
    1 + 2 + 3 + 4
    and so on ...
    Leading to n*(n-1)/2 individual additions,
    which is O(n^2)
    """

    cusum = []

    for i in range(len(values)):
        the_sum = sum(values[:i+1])
        cusum.append(the_sum)


    return cusum
```

Listing 2.6: Slow cumulative sum with hidden complexity

Listing 2.6 implements a cumulative sum algorithm in $\mathcal{O}(n^2)$ time by recalculating the sum of the series up to element i at every step of the way. We saw in the previous section how Python's native **sum** is no faster or slower than the same algorithm written in pure Python, so we can be sure that this algorithm is incurring unnecessary complexity by repeatedly summing the series for every i. We say that the **sum** function here introduces hidden complexity because it is not obvious that an expensive loop is occurring inside the call to **sum**. See Listing 2.7 for an equivalent pure-Python implementation of this bad algorithm.

```python
def slow_cusum_expanded(values: List[float]) -> List[float]:
    """
    Same as the above, O(n^2), but exposes the hidden
    complexity of sum()
    """

    cusum = []

    for i in range(len(values)):

        accumulator = 0
        for j in range(i+1):
            accumulator += values[j]
```

```
        cusum.append(accumulator)

    return cusum
```

Listing 2.7: Slow cumulative sum with obvious complexity

Listing 2.7 does the exact same thing as Listing 2.6 in the exact same way, but it exposes the complexity of the algorithm by explicitly using nested **for** loops. We can see in Table 2.2 that the execution speed for these two algorithms is virtually the same, which can be inferred from our discussion in the last section of this chapter.

We have discussed how bad this algorithm is, but we have not discussed what a better version looks like. The better version of this algorithm arises from applying a smidgen of creativity to the problem. We can re-write the cumulative sum equation as follows.

$$y_i = y_{i-1} + x_i$$

for $i \in 2, ..., n$, while $y_1 = x_1$. Thinking about the relationship between x and y in this way gives rise to a much more efficient implementation of the algorithm. The version in Listing 2.8 performs n additions instead of $(n^2 - n)/2$ additions.

```python
def python_fast_cusum(values: List[float]) -> List[float]:
    """
    This is O(n) time, because it does n additions for n
    values
    """
    cusum = []
    accumulator = 0

    for value in values:
        accumulator += value
        cusum.append(accumulator)

    return cusum
```

Listing 2.8: Pure Python fast cumulative sum

See Listings 2.9, 2.10, and 2.11 for **pandas**, **numba**, and **numpy** implementations of this algorithm. These implementations have similar performance profiles to those of the vanilla sums.

```python
def pandas_fast_cusum(values: pd.Series) -> pd.Series:
    """
    This is O(n) and optimized with C code
    """
    return values.cumsum()
```

Listing 2.9: pandas fast cumulative sum

```python
@jit(nopython=True)
def _numba_fast_cusum(values: np.ndarray) -> np.ndarray:
    """
    This is O(n) time and just-in-time compiled with numba
    """
    cusum = np.zeros(values.shape[0])
    accumulator = 0

    for index, value in enumerate(values):
        accumulator += value
        cusum[index] = accumulator

    return cusum


# Get numba to run the jit optimization
_numba_fast_cusum(np.random.random(100000))

def numba_fast_cusum(values: np.ndarray) -> np.ndarray:
    return _numba_fast_cusum(values)
```

Listing 2.10: numba fast cumulative sum

```python
def np_fast_cusum(values: np.ndarray) -> np.ndarray:
    """
    This is O(n) and optimized with C code
    """
    return values.cumsum()
```

Listing 2.11: numpy fast cumulative sum

See Table 2.2 for execution times on these algorithms.

f	n	t (ms)	n/t
slow_cusum	1E+04	4.4E+03	2.3E+00
slow_cusum_expanded	1E+04	6.4E+03	1.6E+00
python_fast_cusum	1E+08	1.1E+04	9.0E+03

f	n	t (ms)	n/t
pandas_fast_cusum	1E+08	8.4E+02	1.2E+05
numba_fast_cusum	1E+08	2.5E+02	4.0E+05
np_fast_cusum	1E+08	3.7E+02	2.7E+05

Table 2.2: Cumulative sum profiles

2.3 Moving Averages

The next layer of complexity involves what are referred to as rolling, windowing, or moving functions. These terms all mean the same thing, and they imply that the output value y_i is a transformation on values of x_i occurring before, after, or around i. The moving average is the simplest example of a non-trivial windowing function. The m period trailing moving average y_i is the average of x_i from $i - m + 1$ through i. The formula is as follows.

$$y_i = \frac{1}{m} \sum_{j=i-m+1}^{i} x_j$$

The ways in which we can express moving averages inefficiently are very similar to the ways in which we can express cumulative sums inefficiently. The complexity of the inefficient implementation of a moving average is $\mathcal{O}(nm)$, because we needlessly take the average of m values at each step of the loop of length $n - m + 1$. See Listing 2.12 for this implementation. Our discussion of hidden complexity in the previous section makes it clear that the **sum** step inside the loop is the cause of the inefficiency.

```python
def slow_moving_avg(values: List[float],
    m: int=20) -> List[float]:
    """
    This is O(nm) for a list of length n because it
    re-computes the average at each step
    """

    # Exit early if m greater than length of values
    if m > len(values):
        return [None] * len(values)
```

```
# Pad initial m-1 values with Nones
moving_avg = [None] * (m-1)

# Compute the moving average
for i in range(m-1, len(values)):
    the_avg = sum(values[(i-m+1):(i+1)]) / m
    moving_avg.append(the_avg)

return moving_avg
```

Listing 2.12: Slow moving average

See Listing 2.13 for an efficient implementation of a moving average in pure Python. The mathematical justification is as follows.

Define a value v_i that represents the trailing moving sum of x_i.

$$v_i = \sum_{j=i-m+1}^{i} x_j$$

Note that $y_i = v_i/m$. By taking the lagged difference of v_i, we can re-write the moving average equation as the following.

$$v_i - v_{i-1} = x_i - x_{i-m}$$

Shifting v_{i-1} around and dividing both sides by m, we get the following.

$$y_t = \frac{v_i}{m} = \frac{1}{m}(v_{i-1} + x_i - x_{i-m})$$

This equation provides an algorithmically efficient method for calculating y_t as in Listing 2.13. See Table 2.3 for the efficiency of these algorithms. Notice that the difference in computation time between the $\mathcal{O}(n)$ version and the $\mathcal{O}(nm)$ version is not in the slope of the line but in vertical distance between the lines. This is because the ratio of the number of operations performed by the slow algorithm to the number of operations performed by the fast algorithm converges as $n \to \infty$ for constant m. In this example, the slow algorithm is about 16 times slower than the fast algorithm for $m = 100$.

```python
def fast_moving_avg(values: List[float],
    m: int=20) -> List[float]:
    """
    This is O(n) for a list of length n because it
    uses the differential of the accumulator at each step
    """

    # Exit early if m greater than length of values
    if m > len(values):
        return [None] * len(values)

    # Pad initial m-1 values with Nones
    moving_avg = [None] * (m-1)

    # Compute the initial values
    accumulator = sum(values[:m])
    moving_avg.append(accumulator / m)

    # Loop through the remainder of the data
    for i in range(m, len(values)):

        # Subtract the out-of-window value
        accumulator -= values[i-m]

        # Add the new in-window value
        accumulator += values[i]

        # Store the average
        moving_avg.append(accumulator / m)

    return moving_avg
```

Listing 2.13: Pure Python fast moving average

As of the time of writing **numpy** does not have a built-in functionality for moving averages, so we will have to get creative with our use of the **np.cumsum** function. Define q_i as the cumulative sum of x_i. From here, we can derive v_i in terms of q_i to get the following given m for $i > m$.

$$v_i = q_i - q_{i-m}$$

We can translate this into **numpy** using the **np.cumsum** function to get the entire vector v_i in one shot, after which we can perform the calculation in Listing 2.13 on it to get the moving average. See Listing 2.14 for a **numpy** implementation of a fast moving average.

```python
def np_fast_moving_avg(values: List[float],
    m: int=20) -> List[float]:
    """
    Calculate the moving average in numpy in O(n) time.
    Calculate v_i in advance using lagged difference of the
    cumsum.
    """

    # Calculate the cumulative sum to derive v_i from
    cumsum = np.cumsum(values)

    # Initialize empty array
    moving_avg = np.empty((len(values),))

    # Fill it with results
    moving_avg[:m-1] = np.nan

    if m <= values.shape[0]:
        moving_avg[m-1] = cumsum[m-1] / m

    if m < values.shape[0]:
        moving_avg[m:] = (cumsum[m:] - cumsum[:-m]) / m

    return moving_avg
```

Listing 2.14: numpy fast moving average

As you might have been able to guess, this implementation is faster than the pure Python implementation because it is vectorized. The one drawback this algorithm could potentially have over the pure Python implementation is that it uses more memory by holding both **cumsum** and **moving_avg** in memory at the same time. This could potentially be optimized away, but we are not dealing with sufficiently large data or sufficiently small RAM to worry about that right now.

The **pandas** module has a built-in interface for applying arbitrary functions on a rolling basis via **pd.Series.rolling**. See Listing 2.15 for the implementation.

```python
def pd_fast_moving_avg(values: pd.Series,
    m: int=20) -> pd.Series:
    """

    This is O(n) time and utilizes pandas .rolling interface
    """

    return values.rolling(m).mean()
```

Listing 2.15: pandas fast moving average

Generic `.rolling` interfaces across many languages have a history
of hiding inefficiencies by repeatedly applying functions to the win-
dow without the necessary optimization. I have not read through
the source code of the **pandas** rolling interface, nor do I fully understand how **pandas**'s native `.mean()` function interacts with it,
but I can at least say that it is not an $\mathcal{O}(nm)$ algorithm like our
slow pure-Python implementation. The `pd.Series.rolling.mean`
function is an $\mathcal{O}(n)$ algorithm, but it is not as fast as it could be.
See Listing 2.16 for a **pandas** moving average algorithm that is
about 3 times faster on large datasets.

```python
def pd_faster_moving_avg(values: pd.Series,
    m: int=20) -> pd.Series:
    """

    This is O(n) time an outperforms the .rolling variant
    """

    cumsum = values.cumsum()
    return (cumsum - cumsum.shift(m)) / m
```

Listing 2.16: pandas faster moving average

The only lesson to be learned here is that it is good to have a
lot of arrows in your quiver. When you know how an algorithm
works, you can profile libraries against alternative implementations
in the same library and often arrive at a better result. For example,
pandas has baked in a lot of relevant and helpful functionality for
time series, and we as developers might want to rely on it when
we are developing that type of software, even if it is not the fastest
thing available. So, once we have made the decision to rely on
pandas, we can still search for optimizations within the library
itself. It is interesting to point out that switching from Listing
2.15 to Listing 2.16 when computing moving averages in **pandas**
would outperform a multi-threaded version of Listing 2.15 on a 4-
core machine. I mention this because developers often make the
mistake of multi-threading things before attempting to optimize

them.

We will move on to discuss the **numba** implementation of this algorithm. Readers that have been following the whole chapter up to this point can probably guess what the **numba** implementation looks like. It is a strange mix between the pure-Python version and the **numpy** version that relies on **numpy** for data types. See Listing 2.17.

```python
@jit(nopython=True)
def _numba_fast_moving_avg(values: np.ndarray,
    m: int=20) -> np.ndarray:
    """
    This is O(n) time and just-in-time compiled with numba
    """

    # Initialize arrays to store data
    moving_avg = np.empty(values.shape)
    moving_avg[:m-1] = np.nan

    # Exit early if m greater than length of values
    if m > values.shape[0]:
        return moving_avg

    # Compute the initial values
    accumulator = np.sum(values[:m])
    moving_avg[m-1] = accumulator / m

    # Loop through the remainder of the data
    for i in range(m, values.shape[0]):

        # Subtract the out-of-window value
        accumulator -= values[i-m]

        # Add the new in-window value
        accumulator += values[i]

        # Store the average
        moving_avg[i] = accumulator / m

    return moving_avg

# Get numba to run the jit optimization
```

```
_numba_fast_moving_avg(np.random.random(100000))

def numba_fast_moving_avg(values: np.ndarray,
    m: int=20) -> np.ndarray:
    return _numba_fast_moving_avg(values, m=m)
```

Listing 2.17: numba fast moving average

Finally see Table 2.3 for the execution time comparisons. The **numba** implementation wins by a large margin.

We will move on to discuss the more general concept of filter operations in the next section. We will learn that there are certain constraints regarding arbitrary filter operations that make them hard to optimize past $\mathcal{O}(nm)$ time. Moving averages are a special case of a filter than can be optimized to $\mathcal{O}(n)$ time. Other special cases like this exists, most notably with exponential moving averages.

f	n	t (ms)	n/t
slow_moving_avg	1E+05	9.7E+02	1.0E+02
fast_moving_avg	1E+07	5.8E+03	1.7E+03
np_fast_moving_avg	1E+07	8.5E+01	1.2E+05
pd_fast_moving_avg	1E+07	4.3E+02	2.3E+04
pd_faster_moving_avg	1E+07	1.4E+02	7.0E+04
numba_fast_moving_avg	1E+07	3.5E+01	2.9E+05

Table 2.3: Moving average profiles

2.4 Filters

In this chapter, we started with the very simple task of summing a list of numbers and gradually generalized the methods to cumulative sums and moving averages. There are similarities between these algorithms and large portions of code are shared between them. The final step to generalizing this concept is to think about the moving average as a type of filter, then generalize our approach to any filter.

A filter operation on a series x_i can be defined as any convolution of x_i against a weight vector w_i that produces a series of equal length y_i, where not all elements of y_i need to be defined. In this section, we will focus on filters that utilize a weight vector w_j for $a \leq j \leq b$, where a and b can be any integer. This filter operation on x_i is defined as follows.

$$y_i = \sum_{j=a}^{b} w_j * x_{i+j}$$

In this formulation, y_i is defined for $\max(-a, 0) < i \leq min(n - b, n)$. Further, $m = b - a + 1$ is the length of the weighting vector, $-a$ is the lookback distance, and b is the lookforward distance. Per our example on moving averages, an m-period trailing moving average on x_i would have weighting vector $w_j = \frac{1}{m}$ for $j \in -m + 1, -m + 2, ..., -1, 0$. In other words, $a = -m + 1$ and $b = 0$, where the elements of the weighting vector are constant at $\frac{1}{m}$.

Readers may notice that, in the above formulation, y_i is the dot-product of w_j and a section of x_i. This provides us with the $\mathcal{O}(nm)$ solution for computing arbitrary weighted filters. Taking the dot-product of w_j and x_i is similar to taking the sum or the mean of a section of x_i for each i, which does not provide an $\mathcal{O}(n)$ solution.

It is not possible to arrive at an $\mathcal{O}(n)$ solution for weighted filters of arbitrary size and content, because we cannot make any assumptions about the relationship between the values of y_i. We can, on the other hand, write the fastest possible algorithm to apply an arbitrary weighted filter to x_i. While we are at it, we can build some logic that takes advantage of the shape and content of w_i when possible to deliver faster results.

See Listing 2.18 for a naive implementation of a weighted filter in pure Python. This algorithm is *naive* because it does not take advantage of any potential opportunities for optimization provided by the shape and content of the weighting vector. In the following examples, b will be derived based on a and the dimensions of w.

```python
def naive_filter(values: List[float], weights: List[float],
        a: int) -> List[float]:
    """
    This is O(nm) for a list of length n and weights of
    length m because it makes no assumptions about the
    shape of the weighting vector
```

```python
    """

    n, m = len(values), len(weights)
    b = a + m - 1

    # Exit early if m greater than length of values
    if m > n or -a > n or b > n:
        return [None] * len(values)

    # Front and back padding of series
    front_pad = max(-a, 0)
    back_pad = max(b, 0)

    # Apply front pad
    y = [None] * front_pad

    # Compute the filter
    for i in range(front_pad, n - back_pad):
        accumulator = 0
        for j in range(m):
            accumulator += weights[j] * values[i+j+a]
        y.append(accumulator)

    # Apply back pad
    y.extend([None] * back_pad)

    return y
```

Listing 2.18: Naive weighted filter in pure Python

Listing 2.18 runs in $\mathcal{O}(nm)$ time for m weights and achieves similar performance to the pure-Python slow moving average in Listing 2.12, when parameterized as a moving average. This implementation misses out on a lot of opportunities to optimize cases when the weights of are not unique. If we have m weights, of which p are unique, we can compute p vectors $w_j * x_i$ for $i \in 1, ..., n$ only as many times as we need to, then organize the results in a separate loop. This algorithm will still be $\mathcal{O}(nm)$, because, while we have reduced the number of multiplication operations, the algorithm is still performing approximately nm dictionary lookups and additions. See Listing 2.19 for an implementation.

```python
def smart_filter(values: List[float], weights: List[float],
```

```python
    a: int) -> List[float]:
    """
    This is O(nm) for a list of length n and weights of
    length m. Takes advantage of duplicate weights to save
    calculations.
    """

    n, m = len(values), len(weights)
    b = a + m - 1

    # Exit early if m greater than length of values
    if m > n or -a > n or b > n:
        return [None] * len(values)

    # Front and back padding of series
    front_pad = max(-a, 0)
    back_pad = max(b, 0)

    # Pre-compute scaled values for each unique weight
    unique_weights: Set[float] = set(weights)
    scaled_vectors: Dict[float, List[float]] = dict()
    for w in unique_weights:
        scaled_vectors[w] = [w * v for v in values]

    # Apply front pad
    y = [None] * front_pad

    # Compute the moving average
    for i in range(front_pad, n - back_pad):
        accumulator = 0
        for j, w in enumerate(weights):
            accumulator += scaled_vectors[w][i+j+a]
        y.append(accumulator)

    # Apply back pad
    y.extend([None] * back_pad)

    return y
```

Listing 2.19: Smart weighted filter in pure Python

Listing 2.19 will execute faster than Listing 2.18 if the overhead incurred from the extra memory usage and dictionary lookups does not exceed to the overhead incurred from performing duplicate multiplication operations. This will not always be the case. See Table 2.4 for runtime charts of each function when $p = 1$, where all weights are the same number. Compare these charts to Table 2.5 when $p = m$, where all weights are unique numbers. The overhead incurred from extra memory management and dictionary lookups causes Listing 2.19 to underperform Listing 2.18 when $p = m$.

From here, we will implement both the naive and smart variants in **numpy** to compare their performances. We will forgo **numba** and **pandas** implementations for this section, because their explanation would likely be redundant.

See Listings 2.20 and 2.21 for the naive and smart variants of the filter algorithm in **numpy**. Note how we use the `np.ndarray.dot` function to replace the inner loop in the naive variant.

```python
def numpy_naive_filter(values: np.ndarray,
    weights: np.ndarray, a: int) -> np.ndarray:
    """
    This is O(nm) for a list of length n and weights of
    length m because it makes no assumptions about the
    shape of the weighting vector
    """

    n, m = values.shape[0], weights.shape[0]
    b = a + m - 1

    # Exit early if m greater than length of values
    if m > n or -a > n or b > n:
        return np.array([np.nan]*n)

    # Front and back padding of series
    front_pad = max(-a, 0)
    back_pad = max(b, 0)

    # Initialize the output array
    y = np.empty((n,))

    # Pad with na values
    y[:front_pad] = np.nan
    y[-back_pad:] = np.nan
```

```python
    # Compute the filter
    for i in range(front_pad, n - back_pad):
        y[i] = weights.dot(values[(i+a):(i+a+m)])


    return y
```

Listing 2.20: Naive numpy filter

Note how we use vector addition in the smart version, which results in significant speed gains. Basic mathematical operations on `np.ndarray` objects are vectorized computations, so any opportunity to perform larger vectorized operations creates speedups.

```python
def numpy_smart_filter(values: np.ndarray,
    weights: np.ndarray, a: int) -> np.ndarray:
    """

    This is O(nm) for a list of length n and weights of
    length m. Takes advantage of duplicate weights to save
    calculations.
    """


    n, m = values.shape[0], weights.shape[0]
    b = a + m - 1

    # Exit early if m greater than length of values
    if m > n or -a > n or b > n:
        return np.array([np.nan]*n)

    # Front and back padding of series
    front_pad = max(-a, 0)
    back_pad = max(b, 0)

    # Initialize the output array
    y = np.zeros((n,))

    # Pad with na values
    y[:front_pad] = np.nan
    y[-back_pad:] = np.nan

    unique_weights: Set[float] = set(weights)
    scaled_vectors: Dict[float, np.ndarray] = dict()
    for w in unique_weights:
        scaled_vectors[w] = w * values
```

```
r1, r2 = front_pad, n-back_pad
for j, w in enumerate(weights):
    v = scaled_vectors[w]
    y[r1:r2] += v[(r1+j+a):(r2+a+j)]

return y
```

Listing 2.21: Smart numpy filter

We will take this opportunity to introduce a useful numpy trick that has countless applications in other algorithms. The `np.ndarray.dot` function in numpy is magical and has multiple purposes. Dot products are typically used to describe multiplication between two vectors that results in a single-valued output, but the `np.ndarray.dot` function is also numpy's interface to matrix multiplication. Note that in numpy, multiplying two matrices A and B using the multiplication operator * results in scalar multiplication, which is an associative operation. To perform matrix multiplication on A and B, you either need to run `A.dot(B)` or `B.dot(A)` depending on the desired order of multiplication.

The numpy tweak we are alluding to involves setting up matrices in order to do as much work as possible inside a single call to `np.ndarray.dot`. Matrix multiplication is a highly versatile and highly optimized vectorized operation, but initializing the operation incurs some overhead. Therefore, setting up matrices appropriately to reduce the number of calls to `np.ndarray.dot` to as few as possible almost always provides speedups over calling `np.ndarray.dot` within a loop.

To apply an arbitrary filter to a numeric series, we will define a $n' = n - m + 1$ as the count of the non-null elements of the y_i. Then, we will set up an $n' \times m$ matrix Y' then multiply it by an $m \times 1$ vector of weights W'. The result of $Y'W'$ is an $n' \times 1$ vector that can be inserted into all of the non-null slots of y_i. We will ignore the boundaries a and b in the following equations for simplicity.

$$Y'W' = \begin{bmatrix} y_1 & y_2 & \cdots & y_m \\ y_2 & y_3 & \cdots & y_{m+1} \\ \vdots & \ddots & & \vdots \\ y_{n-m+1} & y_{n-m+2} & \cdots & y_n \end{bmatrix} \begin{bmatrix} w_1 \\ w_2 \\ \vdots \\ w_m \end{bmatrix}$$

See Listing 2.22 for this implementation. This algorithm is still *naive* in the language of this section, because it does not take advantage of duplicate weights to avoid duplicate multiplications. Nonetheless, it is significantly faster than the alternative naive algorithm presented in Listing 2.20. Of all of the filter algorithms discussed in this section, Listing 2.22 seems to be consistently the fasted for $n < 500$. See Tables 2.4 and 2.5.

```python
def numpy_naive_matrix_filter(values: np.ndarray,
    weights: np.ndarray, a: int) -> np.ndarray:
    """
    This is O(nm) for a list of length n and weights of
    length m. Takes advantage of duplicate weights to save
    calculations.
    """

    n, m = values.shape[0], weights.shape[0]
    b = a + m - 1

    # Exit early if m greater than length of values
    if m > n or -a > n or b > n:
        return np.array([np.nan]*n)

    # Front and back padding of series
    front_pad = max(-a, 0)
    back_pad = max(b, 0)

    # Initialize the output array
    y = np.zeros((n,))

    # Pad with na values
    y[:front_pad] = np.nan
    y[-back_pad:] = np.nan

    # Build a matrix to multiply with weight vector
    q = np.empty((n - front_pad - back_pad, m))
```

```
for j in range(m):
    q[:,j] = values[j:(j+n-m+1)]

y[front_pad:-back_pad] = q.dot(weights)

return y
```

Listing 2.22: numpy naive matrix filter

f	n	t (ms)	n/t
naive_filter	1E+06	6.6E+03	1.5E+02
smart_filter	1E+06	5.3E+03	1.9E+02
numpy_naive_filter	1E+07	1.0E+04	9.5E+02
numpy_smart_filter	1E+07	3.1E+02	3.2E+04
numpy_naive_matrix_filter	1E+07	2.5E+03	4.0E+03

Table 2.4: Filter profiles for p=1

f	n	t (ms)	n/t
naive_filter	1E+06	6.5E+03	1.5E+02
smart_filter	1E+06	8.7E+03	1.2E+02
numpy_naive_filter	1E+07	1.1E+04	9.4E+02
numpy_smart_filter	1E+07	6.4E+02	1.6E+04
numpy_naive_matrix_filter	1E+07	2.5E+03	4.0E+03

Table 2.5: Filter profiles for similar p and m

2.5   Discussion

We will wrap up this chapter with the following important notes.

2.5.1   Other Operators

In this chapter, we used simple addition to explore some complex topics in algorithm optimization. We will not have a chapter on multiplying things or subtracting things, because it is safe to say the same principles apply to every basic arithmetic operation. Remember that time complexity focuses on the relative number of core operations you perform in an algorithm. It does not matter much what type of operation you are doing. It only matters that you do it as few times as possible to achieve your desired result.

2.5.2 Magic Methods and Data Structures

I will offer a word of warning here that these methods do not apply to everything in the Python programming language that uses a plus sign. Python offers the *magic method* interface to make classes more intuitive to work with. These magic methods allow programmers to define what happens when certain common operations are run on an object, including initializing, hashing, adding, printing, comparing, and many more. I am bringing this up here to make readers aware that, since objects can define what happens when they are added to each other, they can introduce hidden complexity into addition operations. In other words, not all additions in Python are $\mathcal{O}(1)$.

Listing 2.23 gives a simple example of how magic methods work to overload the addition operator.

```python
class A(object):
    def __init__(self, value: int):
        self.value = value

    def __add__(self, another_value: int):
        return A(self.value + another_value)

a = A(3)
print((a+4).value)
# Returns 7

a = A(8)
a += 9
print(a.value)
# Returns 17
```

Listing 2.23: Magic method for addition

In the above listing, we defined a trivial class A that stores an integer and supports addition against other integers. The point of this illustration is to show just how easy it is for classes to perform arbitrary operations inside magic methods. We could very easily stick a `for` loop inside the `__add__` method to introduce some devious hidden complexity, as in Listing 2.24.

```python
class A(object):
    def __init__(self, value: int):
        self.value = value

    def __add__(self, another_value: int):
        accum = 0
        for _ in range(self.value):
            accum += 1
        for _ in range(another_value):
            accum += 1
        return A(accum)

a = A(3)
print((a+4).value)
# Returns 7

a = A(8)
a += 9
print(a.value)
# Returns 17
```

Listing 2.24: Devious magic method for addition

Although these examples are trivial and funny, they hold important lessons. One of the most commonly abused magic methods for addition has to do with the difference between the following two loops. We will discuss the difference between these two loops later in the book.

```python
x = list()
for i in range(5):
    x += [i]
print(x)
# Returns [0, 1, 2, 3, 4]

x = list()
for i in range(5):
    x.append(i)
print(x)
# Returns [0, 1, 2, 3, 4]
```

Listing 2.25: Two ways to construct a list

2.6 Conclusion

Now that we are done adding things, we will move on to counting things. This simple concept will end up illuminating a lot of very important truths about computer science.

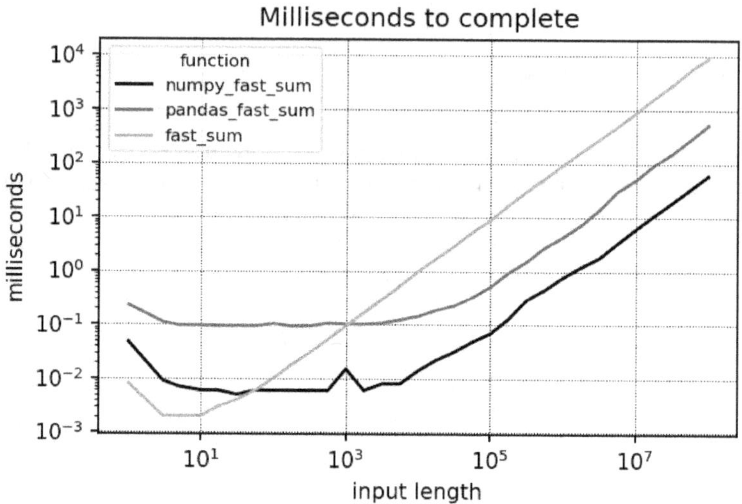

Figure 2.1: Sum execution times

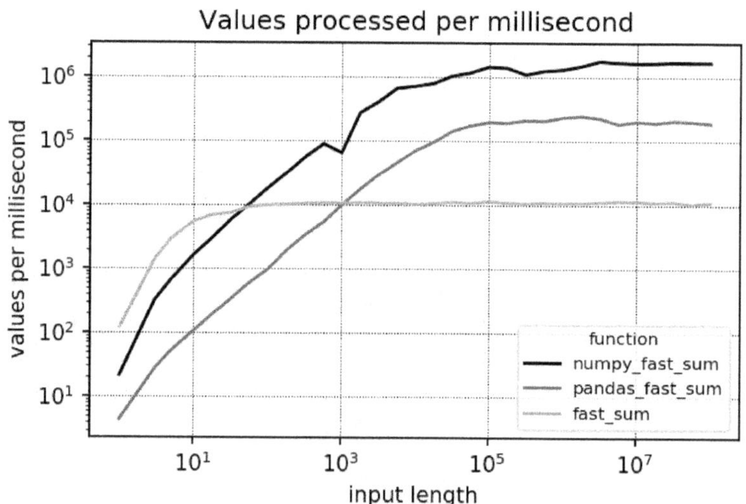

Figure 2.2: Sum efficiencies

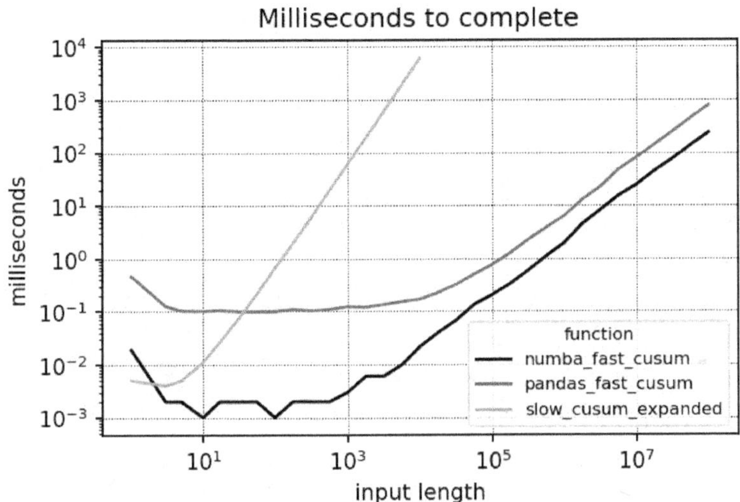

Figure 2.3: Cumulative sum execution times

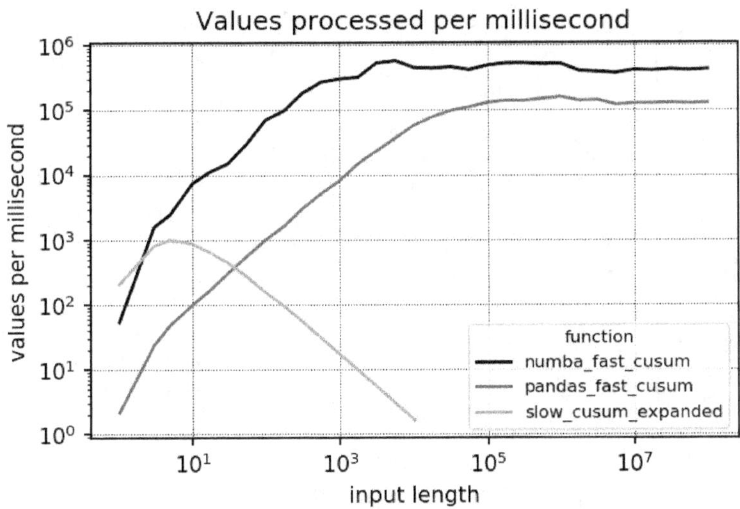

Figure 2.4: Cumulative sum efficiencies

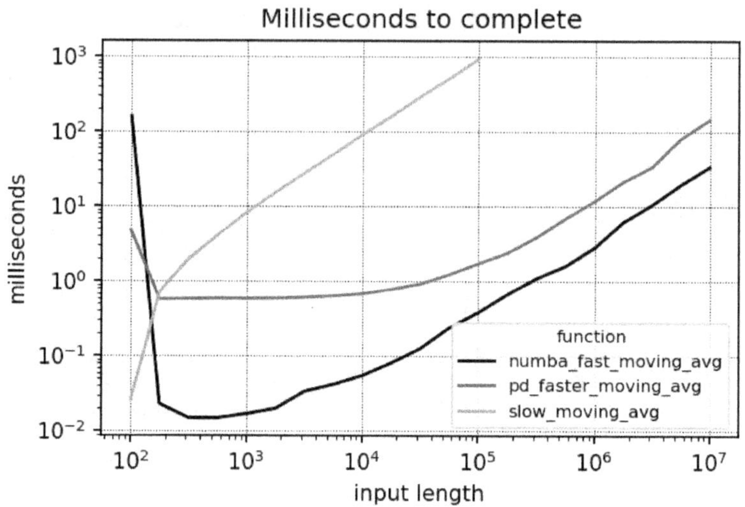

Figure 2.5: Moving average execution times for m=100

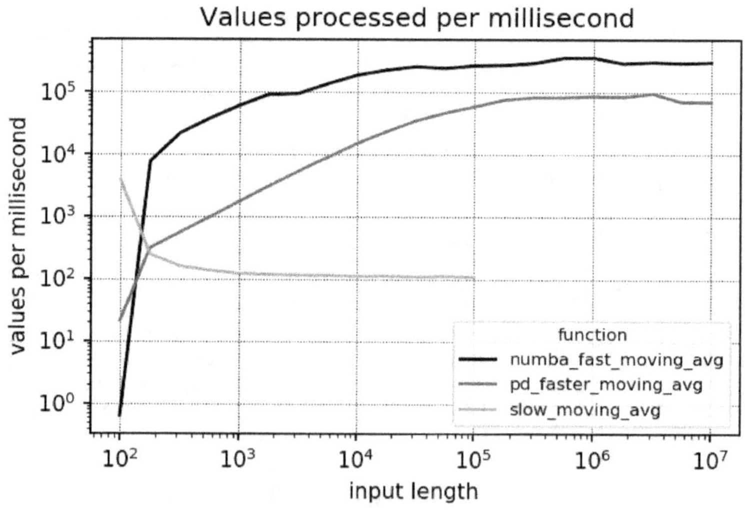

Figure 2.6: Moving average efficiencies for m=100

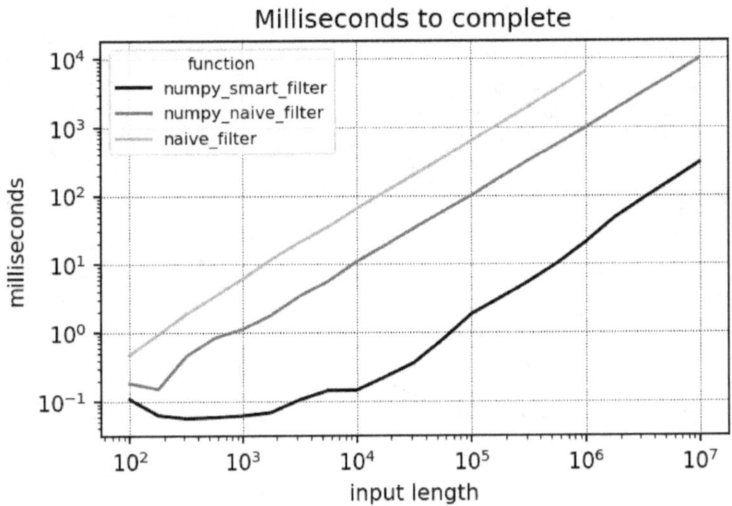

Figure 2.7: Filter execution times for p=1 and m=21

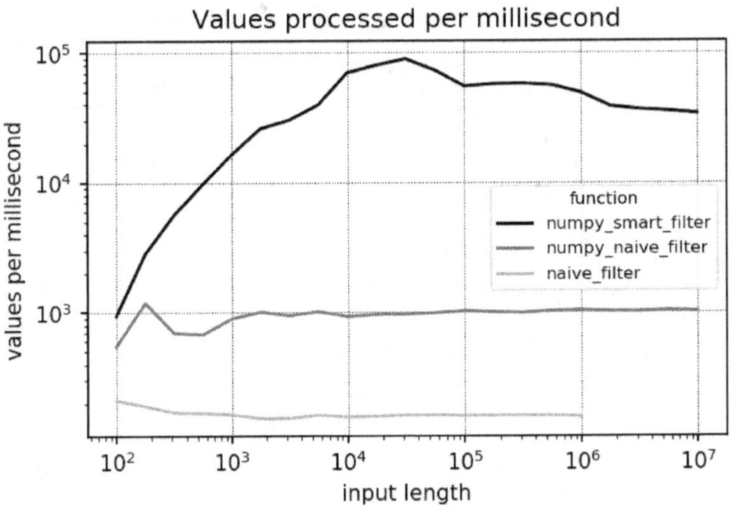

Figure 2.8: Filter efficiency for p=1 and m=21

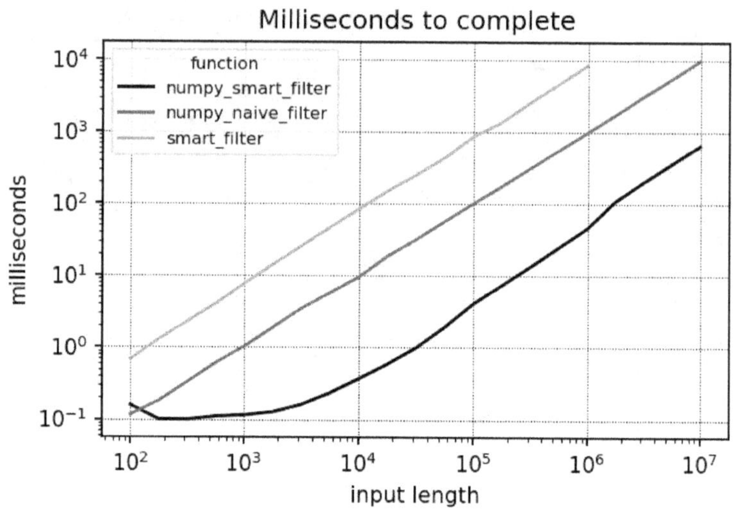

Figure 2.9: Filter execution times for p=m and m=21

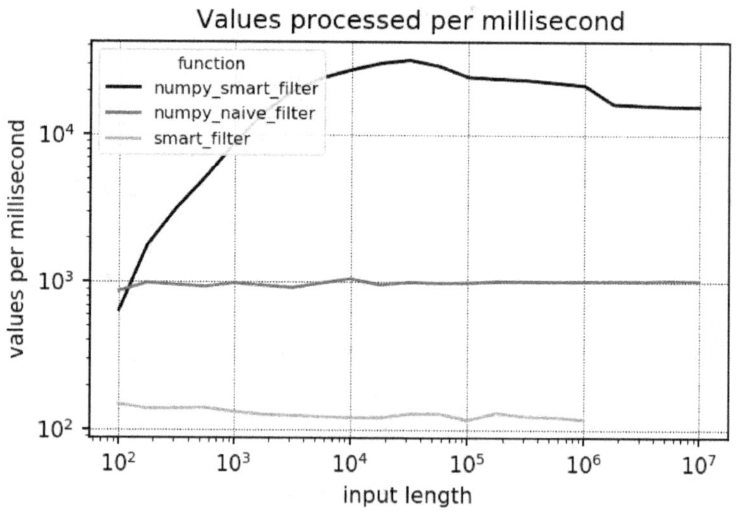

Figure 2.10: Filter efficiency for p=m and m=21

Chapter 3

Counting Things

This chapter is all about counting things. We will talk a lot about hash tables, which Python implements through `dict` and `set` objects. Before we talk about how hash tables work, we will work through a few examples.

3.1 Occurrences of Values

Given a list of things, how can we efficiently count up the number of occurrences of each thing? This is a fundamental and important problem in computer science. In the following examples, we will use random words as things. For example, a random word could be the string `ag4bdjeu`. To test the computational efficiency of our counting algorithms, we will generate millions of random words, then try to count the frequency of each of them.

In the following examples, n will refer to the number of words in the input data, and m will refer to the number of unique words in the input data. Slow algorithms will run in $\mathcal{O}(nm)$ time while fast algorithms will run in $\mathcal{O}(n)$ time. See Listing 3.1 for the slow algorithm.

```python
def slow_count_occurrences(
    the_words: List[str]) -> List[Tuple[str, int]]:
    """
    This algorithm is O(nm) for n total words and m unique
```

```python
    words
    """

    # Our output data structure will be a list of tuples
    count_by_word = list()

    # Get a list of all unique words using set
    unique_words = set(the_words)

    # Loop through unique words
    for word_a in unique_words:

        # Count the occurences
        accumulator = 0
        for word_b in the_words:
            if word_a == word_b:
                accumulator += 1

        # Store the character with the count
        count_by_word.append((word_a, accumulator))

    return count_by_word
```

Listing 3.1: Slow count occurrences

The slow algorithm in Listing 3.1 has $\mathcal{O}(nm)$ complexity because
it performs a comparison between `word_a` and `word_b` a total of
n times for every unique word in the input data. This laborious
series of comparisons would be necessary if we did not have access
to hash tables. See Listing 3.2 for an $\mathcal{O}(n)$ implementation utilizing
hash tables.

```python
def fast_count_occurrences(
    the_words: List[str]) -> Dict[str, int]:
    """
    This algorithm is O(n) for n words
    """

    # Our output data structure
    count_by_word = dict()

    # Loop through the words
    for word in the_words:
```

```python
    # Make sure the dictionary knows about the words
    if not word in count_by_word:
        count_by_word[word] = 0

    # Incriment the counter
    count_by_word[word] += 1

    return count_by_word
```

Listing 3.2: Fast count occurrences

The code in Listing 3.2 is the reason people joke about hash tables being the most magical concept in computer science. This algorithm is still $\mathcal{O}(n)$ despite making multiple calls to Python's **in** operator, because lookups, gets, and sets are all $\mathcal{O}(1)$ operations on hash tables.

Hash tables, in general, are interfaces for managing key-value pairs. Looking up a key return a value. The keys and values themselves can be anything, as long as the keys are hashable. The magical part of hash tables is in the hidden data structure that manages these relationships.

A hash table contains an array-like data structure of indexes that point to the values. The keys are translated into indexes through a hashing function.

We know that array-like data structures are ordered in contiguous memory on your machine. In other words, each index of an array corresponds to a specific memory address (most likely on your RAM) that can be looked up in $\mathcal{O}(1)$ time. Hash tables simply use hashing functions to convert arbitrary objects to locations in contiguous memory. The cost is that a lot of potential memory addresses can be left blank, because the hash table does not know in advance the output values of the hashing function. A potential pitfall is that multiple objects can hash to the same index, causing a collision. Fortunately, brilliant computer scientists have found ways to minimize and circumvent these problems, so we can use our hash tables under the assumption of efficiency and freedom from collisions.

Figure 3.1 shows a schematic of a simple hash table. As we can see in the figure, the hashing function translates the keys to an index of an array, which points to a value. This value

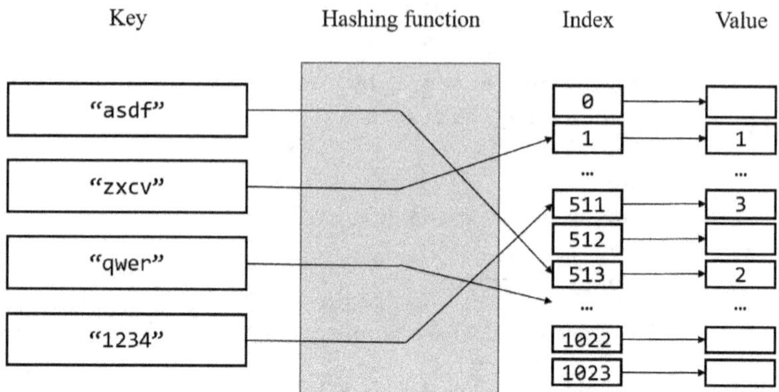

Figure 3.1: Hash table schematic

can be empty for keys that have not been assigned. For example, in Python, if you try to access a key without a value via `some_dictionary['some_empty_key']`, Python will raise a `KeyError`. The assumption when using dictionaries in this fashion is that a lookup call should evaluate to an existing key, otherwise an error has been made. In order to set the value to something, you perform a dictionary assignment via `some_dictionary['some_key'] = some_value`.

In Python, `dict` and `set` objects are hash tables. A `dict` object is a traditional implementation of a hash table. A `set` object can be thought of as a hash table where the values only have two states, existent and non-existent. For both `dict` and `set` objects, the keys are always considered unique. Note Figure 3.1. If there were any duplicates in the "keys" column of Figure 3.1, the two duplicate keys would simply point to the same index. Thus, hash tables have no concept of duplicate keys, and the keys of hash tables can be used to keep track of uniqueness. Python's `set` implementation is an alternative usage of hash tables that serves this express purpose.

Of course, because lookups, gets, and sets are $\mathcal{O}(1)$ for hash tables, the hashing function itself must be $\mathcal{O}(1)$. Hashing functions have complex origins in the field of cryptography. An appropriate hash function for a hash table should be balanced in both evaluation speed and uniqueness, in order to maintain efficiency while avoiding collisions. You can access the hash value for any object in Python using the `hash` function. For example, `hash('some_string')` yields a long integer (-5319524658653967092 on my machine) that would be used to compute the memory location of the value in a `dict` object. Interestingly, `hash(123)` yields `123`, because the input argument is already an integer. It makes perfect sense to make the `hash` function pass-through for integers, because integers already have a notion of uniqueness and order that allows them to be mapped to memory addresses. Understandably enough, the hash of a floating point value is yet another long integer.

The `hash` function in Python can be customized in a class definition via the magic method `__hash__`. So, if the programmer wanted to define a notion of uniqueness for a class and its corresponding objects, he or she could do so by declaring the `__hash__` magic method. The return value of such a method would typically be `hash((self.some_value, self.another_value, ...))`. The concept of magic hashing methods in Python suggests another important fact. The algorithms that hash each built-in type in Python are different. In other words, the string hashing algorithm is some cryptographic algorithm, and the float hashing algorithm is another cryptographic algorithm, and so on.

Not all types in Python are considered *hashable*. For example, if you try to use a list as a key in a dictionary, Python will raise a `TypeError`. It is technically possible to develop a hash function for a list, but that is besides the point. Python enforces this as a matter of best practice. In general, we should only use immutable types as keys in hash tables. Thus, integers, floats, strings, dates, and tuples are all fair game as keys in hash tables.

Now that we understand how hash tables work, we can proceed to discuss other implementations of $\mathcal{O}(n)$ counting algorithms. All of the following counting algorithms will use this hash table method *under the hood*. We know this fundamentally because there is no other known method in computer science to accomplish this task efficiently. Also, our profiling in Table 3.1 and Figures 3.2 and 3.3 confirm it. The only meaningful question that remains would be, "How much faster are they than the pure Python version, and why?"

The documentation for Python's `collections` library has *high-performance container datatypes* in the headline. We will put that to the test in Listings 3.3 and 3.4.

Listing 3.3 implements the fast counting algorithm using

`defaultdict` from the `collections` library. This object is a dictionary-like object that is incapable of raising a `KeyError`. Instead, any time you access a key, if it does not exist, it is defaulted a certain value. A very common design pattern is to declare things like `defaultdict(int)`, `defaultdict(str)`, and `defaultdict(list)`, which correspond to 0, `''`, and `[]` as the default values of the keys. In Listing 3.3, we use `defaultdict(int)` to default the value of our word count to zero. So, instead of checking if the key exists, we can skip that step entirely and just focus on the accumulator.

```python
from collections import defaultdict


def defaultdict_fast_count(
    the_words: List[str]) -> Dict[str, int]:
    """
    This algorithm is O(n) for n words
    """

    # A dictionary whose values default to zero
    count_by_word = defaultdict(int)

    # Loop through the words
    for word in the_words:

        # Incriment the counter
        count_by_word[word] += 1

    return count_by_word
```

Listing 3.3: defaultdict fast count occurrences

Based on the performance profiles in Table 3.1, the `defaultdict` object looks to be slightly slower that the regular `dict` implementation. This suggests that the `defaultdict` class is not optimized beyond the Python level. Rather, it is a Python-level subclass of a `dict` with some unique interface features.

Listing 3.4 shows an implementation with `collections.Counter`. This class is actually optimized below the Python level and outperforms all other implementations in this chapter. The `Counter` is a subclass of a regular `dict` that counts its input arguments and provides a `dict`-like interface to the results. The brevity of Listing 3.4 is sufficient proof that this a well-studied problem in computer science.

```python
from collections import Counter

def counter_fast_count(
    the_words: List[str]) -> Dict[str, int]:
    """
    This algorithm is O(n) for n words
    """

    return Counter(the_words)
```

Listing 3.4: Counter fast count occurrences

There are corresponding solutions to this problem using built-in **numpy** and **pandas** functions. See Listings 3.5 and 3.6. As we learned from earlier implementations of the counting algorithm, the problem of determining the uniqueness of a word and counting its frequency are related in that they both rely heavily on hash tables. The **numpy** implementation exposes this idea further. In **numpy**, the built-in function to count things is a simple modification of the function that returns the unique elements of an array.

```python
def np_fast_count(
    the_words: np.ndarray) -> Tuple[np.ndarray, np.ndarray]:
    """
    This algorithm is O(n) for n words
    """

    return np.unique(the_words, return_counts=True)
```

Listing 3.5: numpy fast count occurrences

The **pandas** implementation relies on the `pd.Series.value_counts()` method, which is an interface to a common form of categorical summary statistic. This function supports a number of arguments that modify the way it displays the results.

```python
def pd_fast_count(
    the_words: pd.Series) -> pd.Series:
    """
    This algorithm is O(n) for n words
    """

    return the_words.value_counts()
```

Listing 3.6: pandas fast count occurrences

See Table 3.1 for speed comparisons. Surprisingly, the Python-based implementations win out by a large margin. I do not have a convincing explanation for this, other than the following. From a computer hardware perspective, not much can be done to vectorize the process of looping through a hash table. Given what we know about hash tables, it makes sense that it not possible to run multiple operations on one simultaneously, thus eliminating the possibility of vectorization.

It might be worth exploring a parallelization of this algorithm. For example, given a massive list of words, we could build k separate counter dictionaries for a k-core computer, then combine the results into a single dictionary by summing all of the values.

See Listing 3.7 for this implementation using the `joblib` library. Table 3.1 includes this result for $k = 8$ on a 10-core computer. The resulting speed is over 10 times slower than its competitors on lists of random words, and the memory usage is very high. Based on our understanding of how hash tables work, it would make sense that this algorithm eats up substantially more memory. This algorithm has to maintain k independent hash tables of counts on the same set of underlying input data, so it would expectedly consume k times as much memory. The cost of memory mapping might be a significant contributor to the slowdown.

The parallel counting algorithm is $\mathcal{O}(n+m)$, assuming k is fixed. In this algorithm, the aggregation step requires looping through about pm keys k times, where p is the average frequency of occurrence of the key in the unaggregated results. When discussing the time complexity of the algorithm, p and k can be dropped as constants. The resulting complexity value reflects that we are running two mostly independent loops that depend on different factors. It also reflects how we can expect the algorithm to increase performance when m is small. Table 3.2 reflects this.

```python
from collections import Counter
from joblib import Parallel, delayed
import math


def _counter_fast_count(
    the_words: List[str]) -> Dict[str, int]:
    return Counter(the_words)


N_JOBS = 8
```

```python
def parallel_fast_count(
    the_words: List[str]) -> Dict[str, int]:
    """
    Count words in parallel using joblib, then aggregate the
    results. This is still O(n+m) complexity for constant k,
    or O(n+km) for variable k.
    """

    # Figure out chunk sizes
    s = chunk_size = math.ceil(len(the_words) / N_JOBS)
    chunk_slices = [(i*s, (i+1)*s) for i in range(N_JOBS)]

    # Set up parallel wrapper and functions
    parallel = Parallel(n_jobs=N_JOBS)
    delayed_count = delayed(_counter_fast_count)

    # Dispatch parallel computation
    counters: List[Dict[str, int]] = parallel(
        delayed_count(the_words[i:j]) for \
        i, j in chunk_slices
    )

    # Aggregate result
    result_count: Dict[str, int] = Counter()
    for counter in counters:
        # Counter.update sums counts
        result_count.update(counter)

    return result_count
```

Listing 3.7: Parallel fast count occurrences

It is worth noting that this is not a highly optimized parallel implementation and other superior implementations may exist. It is also worth noting that Table 3.1 contains profiles of highly dissimilar lists of words. Performance of these algorithms can vary significantly based on the number of keys in the dictionary. Table 3.2 shows profiles of the same algorithms for a larger list of less than 40 unique words.

One of those most interesting results of Table 3.2 is that slow_count_occurrences from Listing 3.1 appears to be $\mathcal{O}(n)$. The slope of the **slow_count_occurrences** line appears to by 1 on the log-log plot, just like the other $\mathcal{O}(n)$ algorithms. Why is this? It is because we are holding m constant. In this profile, the number of unique words is nearly constant and less than 40. Thus, our slow $\mathcal{O}(nm)$ algorithm appears to be growing linearly like its friends. This is a useful lesson in both the utility and danger of profiling our code. First, we must have a solid understanding of computer science principles, then we can start profiling. If we purely profile without understanding computer science, our profiles can lie to us. If we seek speed without knowledge, we are like a mathematician that uses a fancy formula without understanding the proof.

The following section will expand on our knowledge of hash tables by using `set` objects to determine the matches within two lists of words.

f	n	t (ms)	n/t
`slow_count_occurrences`	1E+04	2.7E+03	3.7E+00
`fast_count_occurrences`	1E+07	3.3E+03	3.0E+03
`defaultdict_fast_count`	1E+07	4.4E+03	2.3E+03
`counter_fast_count`	1E+07	2.1E+03	4.7E+03
`np_fast_count`	1E+07	2.8E+03	3.5E+03
`pd_fast_count`	1E+07	9.9E+03	1.0E+03
`parallel_fast_count`	1E+07	4.3E+04	2.3E+02

Table 3.1: Count occurrences (dissimilar words) profiles

f	n	t (ms)	n/t
`slow_count_occurrences`	1E+06	9.8E+02	1.0E+03
`fast_count_occurrences`	1E+08	1.0E+04	9.8E+03
`defaultdict_fast_count`	1E+08	8.4E+03	1.2E+04
`counter_fast_count`	1E+08	5.0E+03	2.0E+04
`np_fast_count`	1E+08	9.8E+03	1.0E+04
`pd_fast_count`	1E+06	6.4E+01	1.6E+04
`parallel_fast_count`	1E+07	1.2E+04	8.3E+02

Table 3.2: Count occurrences (similar words) profiles

3.2 Matches Between Two Lists

This section will detail the problem of determining which elements of one list are also in another list. We learned in the last section how **set** objects are a special type of hash table used to keep track of unique values. In other words, a **set** object is a like a **dict** object with only the keys. If a key of that hash table hashes to a non-empty value, it is considered to be in the set. If a key in that hash table hashes to an empty value, it is considered to not be a part of a set.

The word *set* comes from the mathematical definition that refers to a collection of values with some property. For example, in mathematical terms, $\{1, 3, 5, 7\}$ represents the set of all odd whole numbers less than 8. Similarly, in the following examples, we will be computing the set of words that belong to both lists provided to the function.

```python
def very_slow_match_within(first_list: List[str],
    second_list: List[str]) -> Set[str]:
    """
    This algorithm is O(nm) for n total words in the first
    list and m total words in the second list
    """
    words = set()
    for word in first_list:
        if word in second_list:
            words.add(word)

    return words
```

Listing 3.8: Very slow match within

Listing 3.8 is very slow because it loops through the first list in its entirety and searches the second list each time, resulting in nm comparison operations for n and m elements in the first and second list.

The **set** object has a method called `.add()` that can be used to statelessly add elements to it. If the element is not in the set, it is added. If the element is already in the set, nothing happens.

Listing 3.9 presents another variation on the slow algorithm that is slightly faster, because it reduces the number of words in the first

list to only its unique elements before looping through it. This is a
simple logical optimization based on the fact that a word can only
be matched once. Duplicate matches waste operations. We will
keep an eye on this algorithm as we proceed through this section,
because it exhibits interesting behaviors when the number of unique
elements in the first list is small.

```python
def slow_match_within(first_list: List[str],
    second_list: List[str]) -> List[str]:
    """
    This algorithm is O(nm) for n unique words in the first
    list and m total words in the second list
    """

    # Get the unique words
    unique_words = set(first_list)

    words = list()
    for word in unique_words:
        if word in second_list:
            words.append(word)

    return words
```

Listing 3.9: Slow match within

Listing 3.10 is $\mathcal{O}(n+m)$ instead of $\mathcal{O}(nm)$, because it reduces both
lists to unique sets before doing any comparison, and it performs all
lookup operations on sets. Even though the code looks similar to
the previous algorithms, the loop section of the algorithm is $\mathcal{O}(n)$
because set lookups are an $\mathcal{O}(1)$ operation.

```python
def fast_match_within(first_list: List[str],
    second_list: List[str]) -> List[str]:
    """
    This algorithm is O(n + m) for n unique words in the
    first list and m total words in the second list
    """

    # Get the unique words
    first_list_unique_words = set(first_list)
    second_list_unique_words = set(second_list)

    words = list()
```

```
for word in first_list_unique_words:
    if word in second_list_unique_words:
        words.append(word)

return words
```

Listing 3.10: Fast match within

We discussed earlier in this chapter how the concept of a set comes from mathematics. Python has created an interface to **set** objects using a lot of language from mathematics. One such operation is the set intersection, denoted by the "∩" symbol. If we call the first list a set A and the second list a set B, we are computing $A \cap B$ with this algorithm. In Python, set intersection is denoted by the *binary and* operator "**&**". See Listing 3.11 for a one-liner that solves this problem using set intersection.

```
def fast_intersection(first_list: List[str],
    second_list: List[str]) -> Set[str]:
    """
    This algorithm is O(n + m) for n words in the first
    list and m words in the second list.

    This problem boils down to a set intersection.
    """
    return set(first_list) & set(second_list)
```

Listing 3.11: Fast intersection

In the **pandas** ecosystem, indexes are the row-alignment and column-alignment data structures for **pd.DataFrame** and **pd.Series** objects. We will work with **pd.Index** objects briefly here because they are dictionary-like. The **pd.Index** object is dictionary-like because it can perform hash-based lookups on itself in $\mathcal{O}(1)$ time, but it can also have duplicate entries. Internally, **pandas** is storing and managing multiple parallel data structures that allow this to occur seamlessly. These other data structures that are not part of traditional Python **dict** objects are likely to create additional overhead and cause slowdowns, while still maintaining $\mathcal{O}(1)$ complexity for lookups.

See Listing 3.12 for the same algorithm using **pd.Index** objects with non-unique entries.

```
def pd_naive_index_match(first_list: List[str],
```

```python
    second_list: List[str]) -> List[str]:
    """

    This algorithm is O(n + m) for n words in the first
    list and m words in the second list

    This is to show that pandas indexes are dict-like
    even when the elements are not unique
    """


    # Create a pandas index of of the list as-is
    index: pd.Index = pd.Index(first_list)

    words: List[str] = []
    for word in set(second_list):
        if word in index:
            words.append(word)


    return words
```

Listing 3.12: Pandas naive index intersection

See Listing 3.13 for the same algorithm again using pd.Index objects with unique entries.

```python
def pd_unique_index_match(first_list: List[str],
    second_list: List[str]) -> List[str]:
    """

    This algorithm is O(n + m) for n words in the first
    list and m words in the second list

    This is to show that pandas indexes are dict-like,
    and performance increases for unique elements
    """


    # Create a pandas index from unique elements
    index: pd.Index = pd.Index(set(first_list))

    words: List[str] = []
    for word in set(second_list):
        if word in index:
            words.append(word)


    return words
```

Listing 3.13: Pandas unique index intersection

Finally see Listing 3.14 for the same algorithm using **pandas** native
`pd.Index.intersection` function.

```python
def pd_native_index_match(first_list: List[str],
    second_list: List[str]) -> pd.Index:
    """
    This algorithm is O(n + m) for n words in the first
    list and m words in the second list
    """

    # Create a pandas index from unique elements
    first_index = pd.Index(set(first_list))
    second_index = pd.Index(set(second_list))
    return first_index.intersection(second_index)
```

Listing 3.14: Pandas native index intersection

See Table 3.3 for performance profiles for these algorithms on a
large number of distinct random words. In this profile, the number
of unique words is nearly equal to the total number of words. In
these profiles, Python's native set intersection functionality outperforms every other algorithm.

See Table 3.4 for performance profiles for these algorithms on a
large number of non-distinct random words. In these profiles, the
number of unique words is never greater than 40. In this setup,
the algorithm with named **slow_match_within** outperforms everything else by a wide margin. This is not because we are wrong
about computational efficiency, or because we are bad at computer science. It has to do with the size and shape of our data,
as well as how Python evaluates the **in** operator. Remember the
slow_match_within algorithm is $\mathcal{O}(nm)$ for n unique words in
the first list and m total words in the second list. Somehow, it
outperformed our **fast_intersection** which is $\mathcal{O}(n + m)$ for n
and m total words in each list. This is not intuitive, because
$40 * 1000000 \gg 1000000 + 1000000$.

If we understand how Python evaluates the **in** operator, we
can determine that the number of operations performed by
slow_match_within is actually much less than the alternatives,
given a small number of unique values in the first and second
lists. Python's **in** operator loops through the list to check if
the left-hand argument matches any elements of the right-hand

argument, while utilizing early stopping.

f	n	t (ms)	n/t
very_slow_match_within	2E+04	1.7E+03	1.2E+01
slow_match_within	2E+04	1.7E+03	1.2E+01
fast_match_within	2E+07	4.7E+03	4.2E+03
fast_intersection	2E+07	2.4E+03	8.3E+03
pd_naive_index_match	2E+07	1.5E+04	1.3E+03
pd_unique_index_match	2E+07	2.0E+04	1.0E+03
pd_native_index_match	2E+07	2.0E+04	9.9E+02

Table 3.3: Match within (dissimilar words) profiles

f	n	t (ms)	n/t
very_slow_match_within	2E+05	6.2E+01	3.2E+03
slow_match_within	2E+08	9.7E+02	2.1E+05
fast_match_within	2E+08	1.9E+03	1.0E+05
fast_intersection	2E+08	1.9E+03	1.1E+05
pd_naive_index_match	2E+08	6.5E+03	3.1E+04
pd_unique_index_match	2E+08	1.9E+03	1.0E+05
pd_native_index_match	2E+08	2.1E+03	9.7E+04

Table 3.4: Match within (similar words) profiles

3.3　Early Stopping

Early stopping is a concept in computer programming that involves taking advantage of any opportunity to exit out of function as soon as your know its result. In other words, if a function seeks to answer a single question, you should seek to exit the function and return the answer to that question as soon as you know it. As a practice, it sounds obvious, but you might be surprised at how many unknown opportunities there are to do this in your own code.

In the last section, we observed a very strange result in our profiles where the `slow_match_within` function outperformed all other functions when the lists were comprised of lots of duplicate values. Our hypothesis is that early stopping in Python's native `in` operator allowed the algorithm to finish faster than alternative solutions using hash tables, despite it being less computationally efficient. In other words, the time it took the computer to run all of necessary hashing operations was greater than the time it took to inefficiently search through a list. This section will briefly explore the concept of early stopping to give some insight into why this occurred.

See Listing 3.15 for a naive implementation of Python's **in** operator. Notice how this function checks the equality between the input value and every element of the list. If it finds an equal value, it assigns **True** to the **is_in** flag, thereby switching it away from its default value of **False**. If there were any equal values, the modified version of the flag is returned. This algorithm is $\mathcal{O}(n)$ because it performs n comparison operations.

```python
def naive_in_operator(value: str,
    sequence: List[str]) -> bool:
    """

    Check if a value is in the sequence, naively


    This is O(n) for sequence of length n
    """

    is_in = False
    for other_value in sequence:
        if value == other_value:
            is_in = True
    return is_in
```

Listing 3.15: Naive in operator

See Listing 3.16 for an early stopping implementation of Python's **in** operator. This algorithm is very similar to the above, except that it returns **True** the moment it sees any equal value in the sequence. This is called early stopping. The result will always be the same as the above algorithm, because only one known equality is needed to be certain that **value** is somewhere in **sequence**. Note that this algorithm is still $\mathcal{O}(n)$ because, while it takes advantage of early stopping, we make no assumptions regarding the content of the list.

```python
def early_stopping_in_operator(value: str,
    sequence: List[str]) -> bool:
    """

    Check if a value is in the sequence with early stopping
```

```
    This is O(n) for sequence of length n
    """

for other_value in sequence:
    if value == other_value:
        return True
return False
```

Listing 3.16: Early stopping in operator

If the elements of the list are entirely unique and `value` is not in `sequence`, then this algorithm performs n comparison operations. If the `value` is equal to `sequence[0]`, then it only performs 1 comparison operation.

Consider an example where there are n elements in the list, n' unique elements in the list, there are an equal number of duplicate elements, and `value` is a random element of the list. Further, consider that the elements of `sequence` are randomly ordered. In this setup, the number of steps needed to encounter an early stopping situation follows a geometric distribution with probability $p = 1/n'$. In other words, the probability of encountering an early stopping situation is $1/n'$ at every step of the loop. Further, the average number of comparisons needed to achieve an early stop is n'. Note how p is entirely determined by the number of unique values in the list and not at all by the size of the list.

Bear in mind that this algorithm is still $\mathcal{O}(n)$, because we make no assumptions about the type of data in the sequence. A mathematical argument for this goes as follows. Consider the same situation as in the last paragraph, except that there is an unknown probability q that `value` is in `sequence`. Under this setup, the average number of operations needed to evaluate the `in` operator is $N = qn' + (1 - q)n$.

To prove that the early stopping algorithm is still $\mathcal{O}(n)$, we simply have to prove that $N < Mn$ as $n \to \infty$ for some arbitrary constant M. Since $0 \leq q \leq 1$ and $n' \leq n$, we can make the following argument for $M = 1$.

$$qn' + (1 - q)n \leq qn + (1 - q)n \leq n \leq Mn$$

For sake of completeness, Listing 3.17 shows the native Python `in` operator. As we will see in the following profiles, the native `in` operator is early-stopping.

```python
def native_in_operator(value: str,
    sequence: List[str]) -> bool:
    """
    Use Python's native in operator to check if a value is
    in a sequence

    This is O(n) for sequence of length n
    """
    return value in sequence
```

Listing 3.17: Native Python in operator

See Table 3.5 for profiles of these functions. In these profiles, the list is comprised of random words with a very low number of duplicates, and the value is set to the 10000-th element of the list. If the list is shorter than 10000 elements, then the value is not an element of it. For the early stopping algorithm and the native in operator, the evaluation time levels off after $n = 10000$ due to early stopping.

Figures 3.10 and 3.11 more or less prove that Python's native in operator is early stopping. Further, they explain the curious behavior in Table 3.4. In those profiles, the overhead incurred by hash tables was more significant than the inefficiencies incurred by list searches. The list searches were able to compete with the hash tables on small numbers of unique values because they took advantage of early stopping.

f	n	t (ms)	n/t
naive_in_operator	1E+07	2.8E+02	3.6E+04
early_stopping_in_operator	1E+07	3.0E-01	3.4E+07
native_in_operator	1E+07	2.0E-01	4.9E+07

Table 3.5: Early stopping profiles

3.4 Lines in a File

For some reason or another, we frequently need to count the number of lines in a file. When dealing with really large files, we might not be interested in parsing or manipulating the data when counting the lines. Maybe we just need to count the number of lines in order to split it up into smaller pieces, or maybe we need to merge multiple large files together in some way. In any case, lets try to do this as fast as possible in Python. Once again, digging deep into seemingly simple tasks will reveal some very interesting truths about computer science.

The key to counting the number of lines in a file will be to do as little processing on it as possible. Typically, data scientists working with CSV files are familiar with **numpy** and **pandas** tools for reading files into arrays and data frames, so they will try something like Listing 3.18 or 3.19 in order to count the lines.

```python
def np_naive_count_lines(filepath):
    """
    Counts lines by parsing file into a numpy array
    """
    data = np.genfromtxt(
        filepath,
        delimiter=',',
        skip_header=True
    )
    return data.shape[0]
```

Listing 3.18: numpy naive line count

By this point in the book, you probably know that any function with the word *naive* in it is a bad one. These two functions are very slow at counting lines compared to available alternatives. Not only do they read the whole file into memory, they perform tons of pre-processing and sniffing on the file in order to guess things like structure, data types, and headers. Finally, the resulting data structures they construct are way larger than necessary for the purpose of counting lines.

```python
def pd_naive_count_lines(filepath):
    """
    Counts lines by parsing file into a pd.DataFrame
    """
    df = pd.read_csv(filepath)
    return df.shape[0]
```

Listing 3.19: pandas naive line count

Further, doing any pre-processing on the file should be considered a waste of time. Python's **csv** module performs equally badly, as in Listing 3.20.

```python
import csv

def csv_slow_count_lines(filepath):
    """
    Counts lines by parsing the csv file line-by-line
    """
    with open(filepath, 'r') as file_ptr:
        csv_reader = csv.reader(file_ptr, delimiter=',')
        line_count = 0
        for row in csv_reader:
            line_count += 1
    return line_count
```

Listing 3.20: Python csv library line count

The art of counting lines is another area where pure Python will
outperform all else, because we can go to great lengths to make
sure Python does as little as possible with the file content. See
Listing 3.21 for an alternative using basic file I/O operations. The
`.readlines()` function is another really common one in data analysis, because it reads the entire file into memory as a list of strings.
This outperforms all of the aforementioned functions by a large
margin simply because it assumes nothing about the content of
the file and does no pre-processing on it.

```python
def slow_count_lines(filepath):
    """
    Counts lines by reading entire file into memory as a
    list of lines represented by strings
    """
    with open(filepath, 'r') as file_ptr:
        lines: List[str] = file_ptr.readlines()
        line_count = len(lines)
    return line_count
```

Listing 3.21: Pure Python slow line count

In Listing 3.21, we are already doing virtually nothing with the
content of the file. So, how can we speed it up even more? The
answer involves using as little memory as possible. Since a string
takes up less memory than an equivalent list of strings, let us try
Listing 3.22 for an even faster solution. The `.read()` function
simply reads the content of the file into a variable as a string. Since
this string can get relatively massive, it will certainly provide a

memory efficiency advantage over Listing 3.21.

```python
def medium_count_lines(filepath):
    """
    Counts lines by reading entire file into memory as a
    string then counting line breaks
    """
    with open(filepath, 'r') as file_ptr:
        file_str: List[str] = file_ptr.read()
        line_count = file_str.count('\n')
    return line_count
```

Listing 3.22: Pure Python medium line count

Listing 3.22 packs the contents of the file into as small of an object as possible, a string, thereby minimizing the memory footprint required to search through it. In order to make this algorithm even faster, we have to concentrate on not reading the contents of the file into memory at all.

Listing 3.23 uses a special property of Python's file-like objects to iterate through the file line-by-line without reading it into memory. For certain file-like objects in Python, the `__iter__` magic method iterates through the file by returning it line by line. At every step of this loop, we are only reading the current line into memory as a string. This is faster than the previous algorithm because the computer never has to read the whole file into memory as a single string. Additionally, each line of the file is read directly from the disk.

```python
def fast_count_lines(filepath):
    """
    Counts lines by iterating through the file directly from
    the disk, reading each line in one at a time
    """
    with open(filepath, 'r') as file_ptr:
        line_count = 0
        for line in file_ptr:
            line_count += 1

    return line_count
```

Listing 3.23: Pure Python fast line count

Listing 3.23 avoids reading the whole file into memory at once by reading it in line-by-line directly from the disk. Still, the contents of the file are being iteratively loaded into memory into the `line` variable. If we can somehow avoid reading any strings into memory, we could get a faster algorithm. Listing 3.24 achieves this through an obscure operating system feature known as memory mapping.

Memory mapping involves virtually constructing a contiguous piece of memory that maps directly to a congruent block of data on the disk. The result is equivalent to the previous algorithm, except that the content of the line is never read into memory. At each iteration of the `while` loop in Listing 3.24, Python checks if there are more than zero byte-characters at a location in the file following a newline character \n. It does so directly on the disk, thereby never really reading a whole line of string data into memory.

```python
import mmap


def fast_mem_map_count(filename):
    """
    Create a memory-mapping in order to count the lines
    """
    with open(filename, 'r+') as file_ptr:
        memory_map = mmap.mmap(file_ptr.fileno(), 0)
        line_count = 0
        while memory_map.readline():
            line_count += 1
    return line_count
```

Listing 3.24: Pure Python memory map fast line count

Note that the behavior of the `mmap` module is dependent on your operating system. These profiles were run a Linux machine. Also note that the results of these profiles will differ between solid state disks (SSDs) and spinning hard disk drives (HDDs). Some of the fastest algorithms might even be slower if your HDD is segmented in such a way that memory mapping is not trivial. These profiles were run on a computer with an SSD.

f	n	t (ms)	n/t
`slow_count_lines`	1E+07	2.8E+03	3.5E+03
`csv_slow_count_lines`	1E+07	2.1E+04	4.7E+02
`medium_count_lines`	1E+07	2.4E+03	4.2E+03
`fast_count_lines`	1E+07	1.8E+03	5.7E+03

f	n	t (ms)	n/t
`fast_mem_map_count`	1E+07	1.2E+03	8.3E+03
`np_naive_count_lines`	1E+06	1.0E+04	9.6E+01
`pd_naive_count_lines`	1E+06	1.4E+03	7.3E+02

Table 3.6: Counting lines in a file

When working through these examples in the GitHub repo, you will not have access to the massive files used to run these profiles GitHub limits the size of uploaded files to 100MB, so you will have to run the `generate_numeric_csv_files.py` script if you want larger data to run profiles against. The largest file generated by that script is about 2GB.

3.5   Occurrences of a Value

Readers may think they are properly equipped to answer this question, because it sounds very similar to questions we have already answered in this chapter. Of course, it is not. In this section, we will be discussing how to count the number of occurrences of a query value in a target data structure. For example, we may want to find the number of times the name *Juliet* appears in the book *Romeo and Juliet*. In optimizing this algorithm, we will end up exposing a lot of interesting capabilities of strings and regular expressions in Python.

The source data for profiling this algorithm will be the complete works of William Shakespeare in a single text file downloaded from https://gutenberg.org. See `data/complete_shakepeare.txt` for the file, which comes in at a whopping 5.5MB. This algorithm will not have profiling charts like the previous ones, because the size of the target data structure is fixed.

See Listings 3.25 and 3.26 for two pure-Python implementations of string counting. The `str.split(value)` method splits the string by the input argument `value` and returns a list. Since the list is split along each occurrence of the string, the total number of occurrences of the string will always be the length of the result minus 1.

```python
def str_split_count(data: str, value: str) -> int:
    """
```

```python
    Return the number of occurrences of value in data by
    splitting data along value into a list
    """
    return len(data.split(value)) - 1
```

Listing 3.25: Pure Python count by string split

Python provides a more direct route to this functionality with the
`str.count(value)` method.

```python
def str_count(data: str, value: str) -> int:
    """
    Simply call python's str.count method
    """
    return data.count(value)
```

Listing 3.26: Pure Python string count

The remaining methods will use the `re` module in Python to execute regular expression searches on the input data. See Listings
3.27, 3.28, and 3.29 for various implementations using the regular
expressions library. We are not doing anything terribly interesting
with these regular expressions. We are simply passing in `value` as
the query string.

```python
def re_subn_count(data: str, value: str) -> int:
    """
    Count the number of substitutions that value word
    perform on data in a regex substitution
    """
    return re.subn(value, '', data)[1]
```

Listing 3.27: Regex substitution count

The `re.subn` function is exactly the same as the `re.sub` function
in that it performs substitutions using regular expressions, but it
also returns the count of substitutions as the second result. Here,
we are simply returning the second result as our solution.

```python
def re_findall_count(data: str, value: str) -> int:
    """
    Count the number of elements returned in an exhaustive
    regex search of value on data
    """
    return len(re.findall(value, data))
```

Listing 3.28: Regex findall count

The `re.findall` and `re.finditer` functions differ only in that the former returns a list of matches and the latter returns an iterator. We test both here in a desperate attempt to save time on memory allocation.

```python
def re_finditer_count(data: str, value: str) -> int:
    """
    Count the number of elements returned in an exhaustive
    regex search of value on data, as an iterator
    """
    return sum(1 for _ in re.finditer(value, data))
```

Listing 3.29 Regex finditer count

See the following tables for results on searching for the word `juliet` and results for searching for the word `the`, which is the most frequently used word in Shakespeare's anthology. The results from this section are not terribly interesting, because Python seems to have handled them pretty well with native string operations.

These profiles are interesting for the purposes of determining the fastest result, but they do not do the functionality and optimizations native to regular expressions any justice. For example, when searching for the word *the*, we undoubtedly picked up many words that contain the same characters, like *thespian* or *aesthetic*. Regular expressions provide us the option to do more complex matching operations, like only matching whole words, while Python's `str.count(value)` method does not.

f	n	t (ms)	n/t
str_split_count	6E+06	6.6E+00	8.4E+05
str_count	6E+06	4.7E+00	1.2E+06
re_subn_count	6E+06	1.0E+01	5.5E+05
re_findall_count	6E+06	2.3E+00	2.4E+06
re_finditer_count	6E+06	4.0E+00	1.4E+06

Table 3.7: Counting occurrences of "Juliet" in Shakespeare

f	n	t (ms)	n/t
str_split_count	6E+06	2.1E+01	2.6E+05
str_count	6E+06	9.7E+00	5.8E+05
re_subn_count	6E+06	3.0E+01	1.9E+05
re_findall_count	6E+06	1.4E+01	4.0E+05

f	n	t (ms)	n/t
re_finditer_count	6E+06	1.6E+01	3.5E+05

Table 3.8: Counting occurrences of "the" in Shakespeare

3.6 Conclusion

So far in this book, we have added things and counted things. In the process of doing these seemingly simple tasks, we have surfaced a lot of interesting problems and created a lot of interesting optimizations. The principles we have discussed so far form a very significant foundation for our understanding of algorithms and high-performance computing.

The next chapter will cover sorting, another cornerstone problem that has received ample attention over the years.

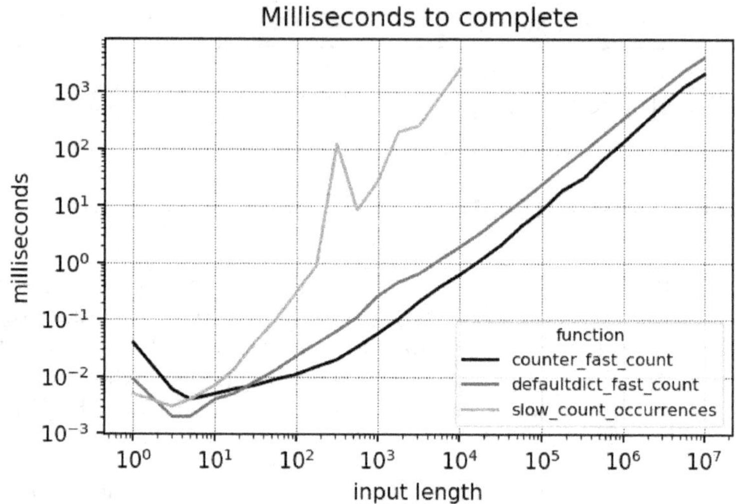

Figure 3.2: Count occurrences execution time (dissimilar words)

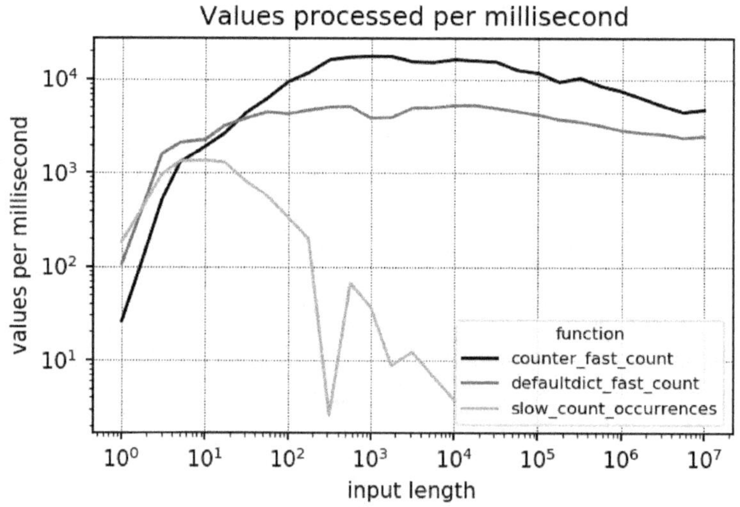

Figure 3.3: Count occurrences efficiency (dissimilar words)

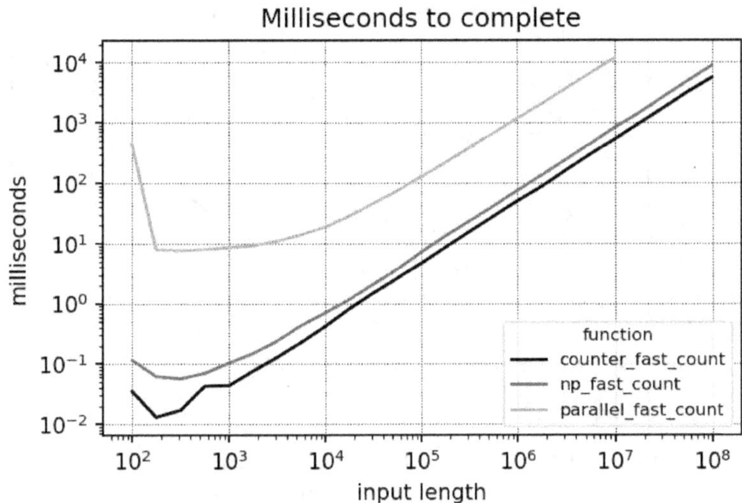

Figure 3.4: Count occurrences execution time (similar words)

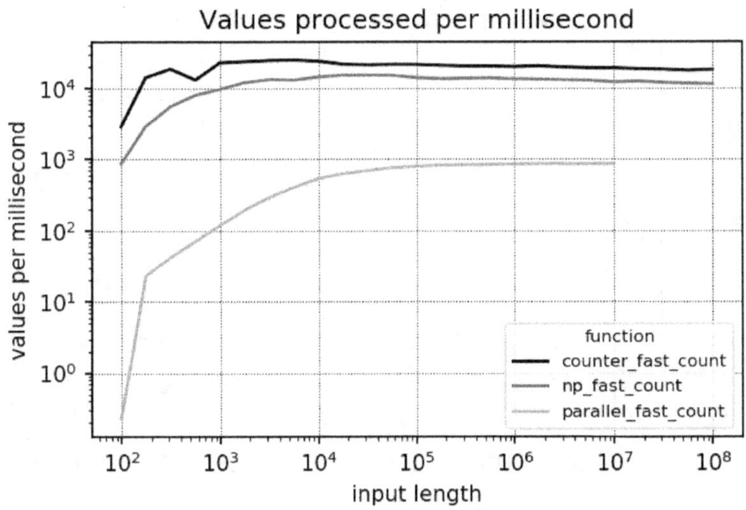

Figure 3.5: Count occurrences efficiency (similar words)

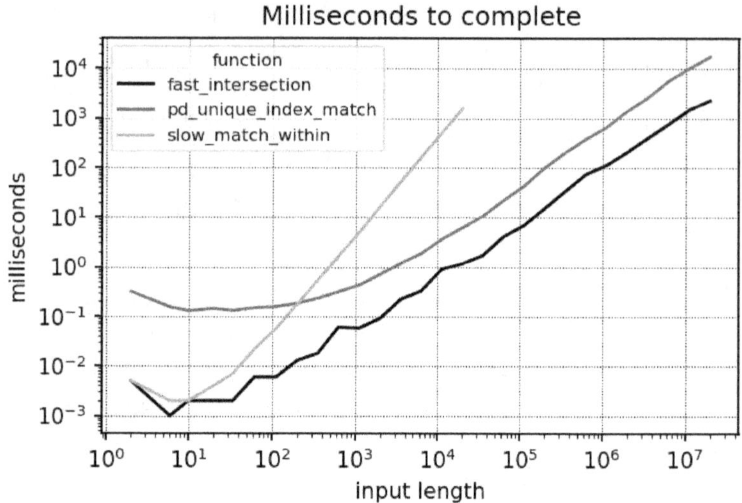

Figure 3.6: Match within execution time (dissimilar words)

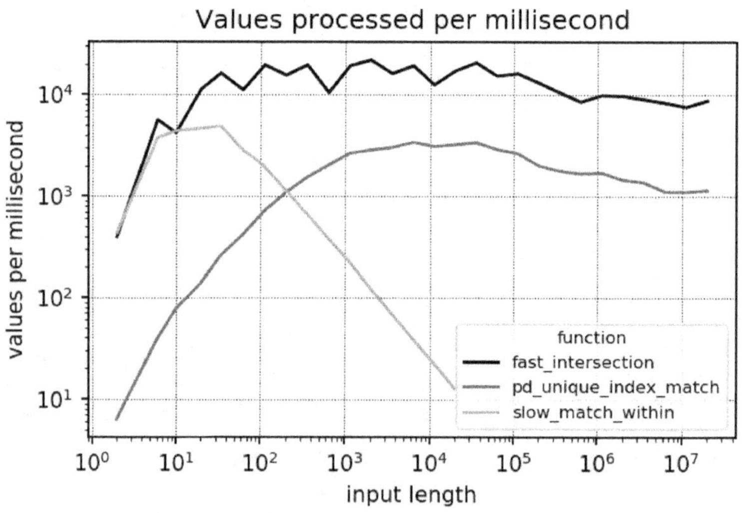

Figure 3.7: Match within efficiency (dissimilar words)

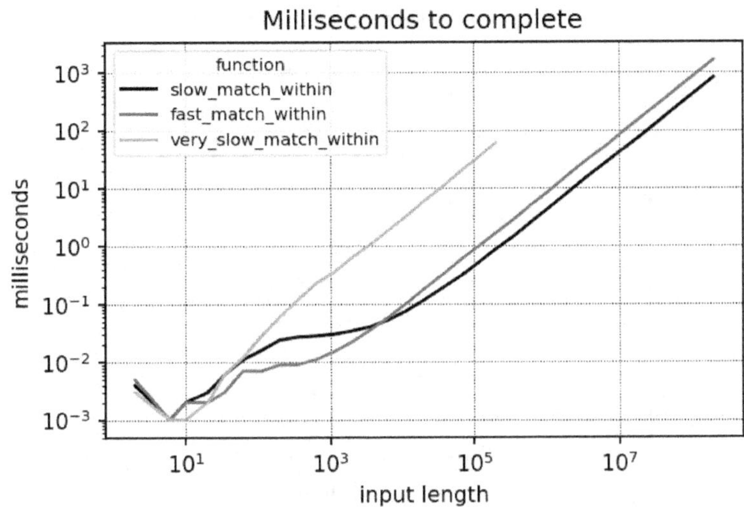

Figure 3.8: Match within execution time (similar words)

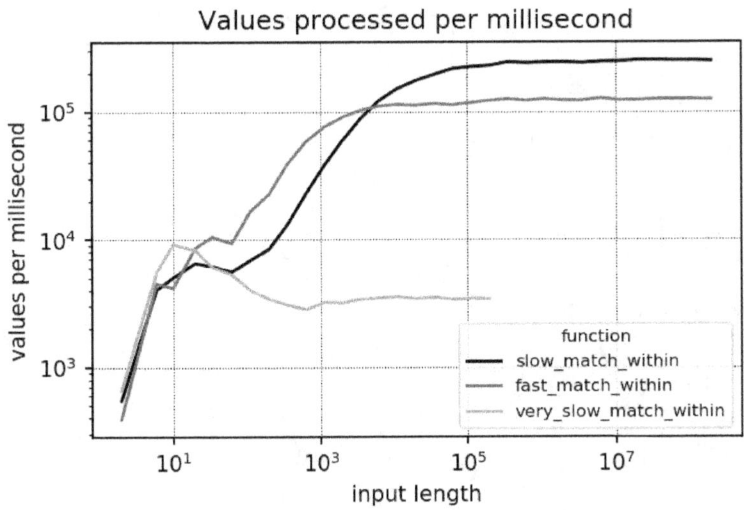

Figure 3.9: Match within efficiency (similar words)

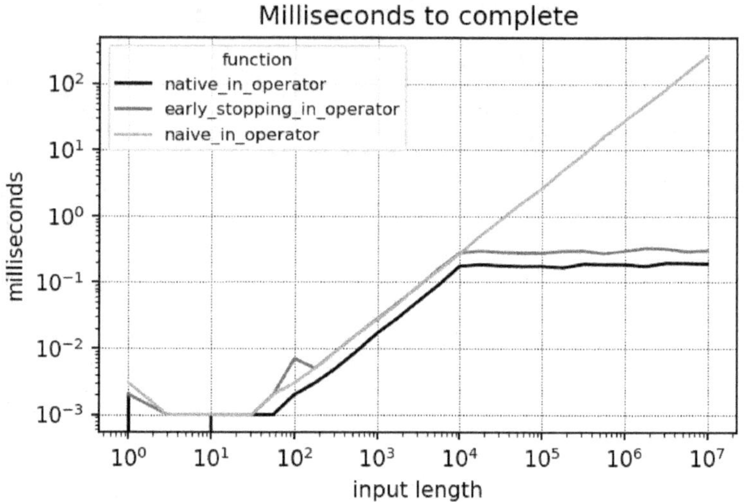

Figure 3.10: In operator execution time (match at 10000)

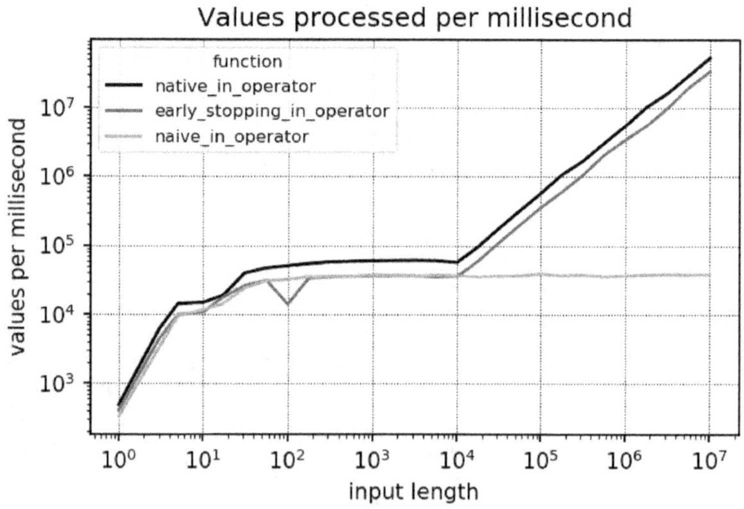

Figure 3.11: In operator efficiency (match at 10000)

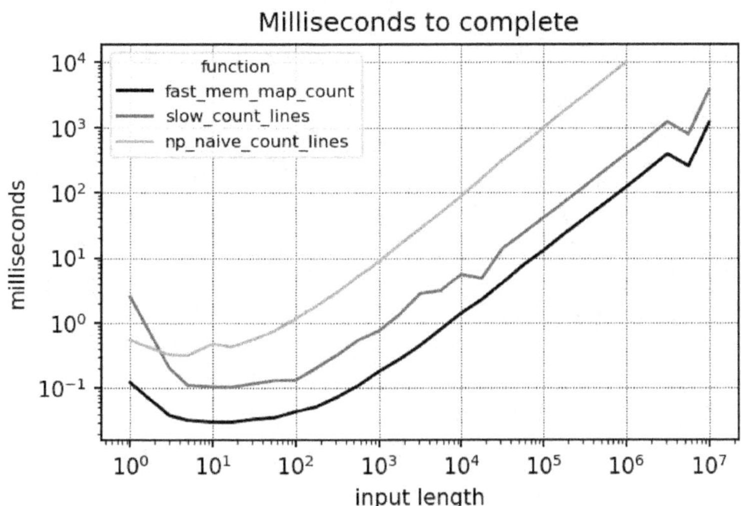

Figure 3.12: Line count execution time

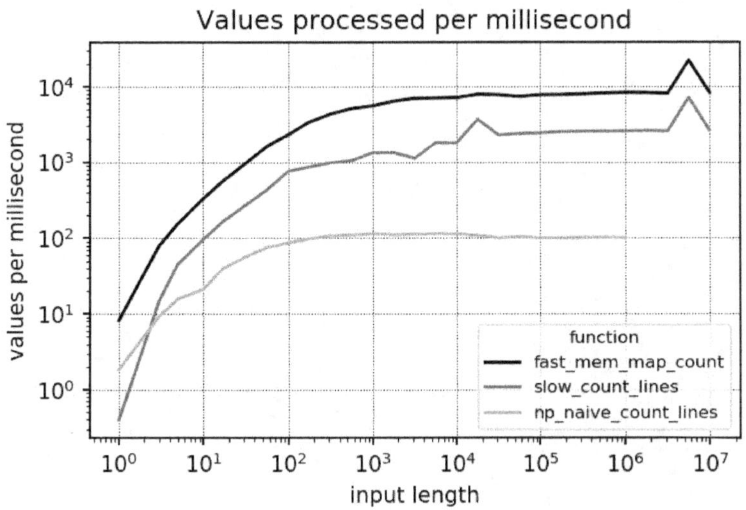

Figure 3.13: Line count efficiency

Chapter 4

Sorting Things

It is rare to see an algorithms textbook that does not come with a thorough and treatment of all of the sorting algorithms developed throughout the course of history. This book is no different.

At the end of the day, you will probably continue to rely on Python's native `list.sort()` functionality when appropriate. We will discuss in this chapter why it continues to be the best choice for general sorting problems. More importantly, we will discuss some foundational data structures, namely binary search trees and max heaps, that are still relevant in many parts of computer science. Understanding these data structures and how they contribute to sorting performance is essential to understanding many algorithms we take for granted every day, including many core features of SQL. We will also explore how certain specific sorting problems can be considerably sped up by using binary search trees and max heaps.

We will start with a theoretical discussion of these data structures before writing any useful code.

When dealing with sorting algorithms, the difference between average-case complexity and worst-case complexity starts to become relevant. Worst-case complexity refers to the worst possible time complexity given a list of input data specifically engineered to slow down a given sorting algorithm. Throughout this chapter, when we refer casually to the *complexity* of algorithms, we will be referring to the average-case complexity.

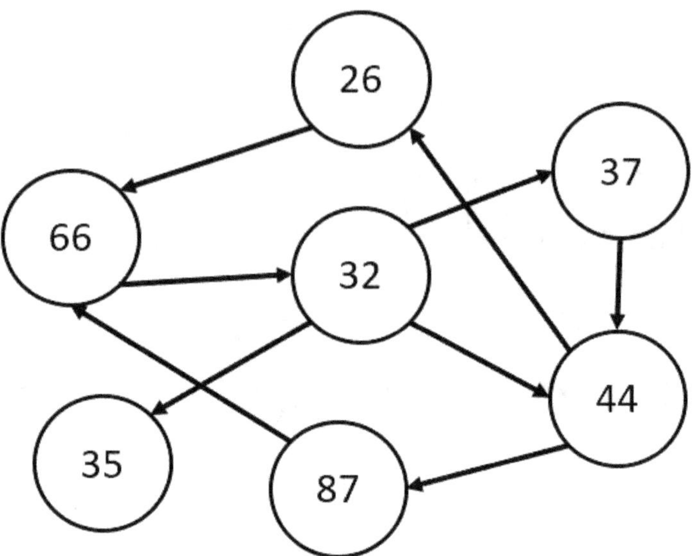

Figure 4.1: Example of a graph

4.1 Graphs, Trees, and Heaps

See Figure 4.1 for a depiction of a graph. A graph, in the most general sense, is a series of nodes connected by edges. In Figure 4.1, *nodes* refers to the circles with numbers, and *edges* refers to the lines. This particular figure happens to be a directed graph, because the lines have arrows indicating which way they point.

Graphs are a mathematical subject that exist separately from computer science. As such, there is no uniformly correct or best way to create a data structure that represents a graph. For example, the directed graph in Figure 4.1 could be represented by a list of the two classes in Listing 4.1, where `node_a` always points to `node_b`.

```python
class Node(object):
    def __init__(value: int):
        self.value = value


class Edge(object):
    def __init__(node_a: Node, node_b: Node):
        self.node_a = node_a
        self.node_b = node_b
```

```
a_node = Node(26)
another_node = Node(66)
some_edge = Edge(a_node, another_node)
...
```

Listing 4.1: Graph data structure example

Alternatively, a graph can be defined in a totally arbitrary and application-specific way. For example, the graph could be defined as a list of tuples of integers, where the first integer points to the second integer, under the assumption that each integer value uniquely represents a node. I think it is important to understand this early on in your education about graphs. A lot of the important algorithms that use these data structures often do so in very creative and unorthodox ways. Most notably, the heap sort algorithm uses a very creative definition of a max heap in order to sort a list of values. We will discuss this in more detail as we proceed.

```
the_graph: List[Tuple[int, int]] = [
    (26, 66),
    (44, 26),
    (37, 44),
    (32, 37),
    ...
]
```

Listing 4.2: Another graph data structure example

4.1.1 Trees

A tree is a directed graph with no cycles where each node has zero or more children. When we say the graph has no cycles, we mean that the arrows only flow from the root node (the top) to leaf nodes (on the bottom). See Figure 4.2 for an example of a tree. The tree in Figure 4.2 is also a *binary* tree, because each node has at maximum two children. Note that a complete binary tree has 2^{i-1} nodes at level i for $i \in 1, ..., n$. Further, the number of levels of a complete binary tree with n nodes is $\log_2(n + 1)$.

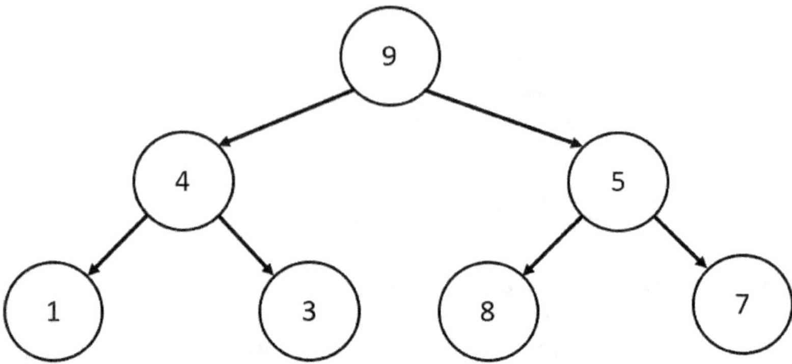

Figure 4.2: Example of a binary tree

4.1.2   Heaps

Binary trees have a lot of interesting properties and special config-
urations that make them helpful in sorting. The first configuration
we will talk about is a *max heap*. A max heap is a tree that satisfies
the *heap property*. The heap property is one of many states of a
heap where every parent node is greater than or equal to its child
nodes. In this configuration, the maximum node is always the root
node. See Figure 4.3 for an example of a max heap. Note how
the nodes below the root do not have any discernible pattern other
than what is guaranteed by the heap property.

To understand why max heaps are useful, we need to understand
a few fundamental operations on heaps. The first fundamental
operation is inserting an element such that the heap property is
maintained. See Figure 4.4 for a step by step example of inserting
the value 99 into the heap. For visualization purposes, pretend the
number 37 was never there to begin with.

To maintain the heap property after an insertion, you have to swap
the inserted node with its parent node if the inserted node is of
greater value. Keep repeating this until the inserted node is less
than its parent, and you have successfully maintained the heap
property. This requires $\lfloor \log_2(n) \rfloor$ comparisons in the worst case for
n total nodes in the tree, but can take as few as 1 comparisons. In
other words, this operation is $\mathcal{O}(\log(n))$.

We are starting to understand how heaps can provide speed advantages to our algorithms. Consider the alternative task of determin-

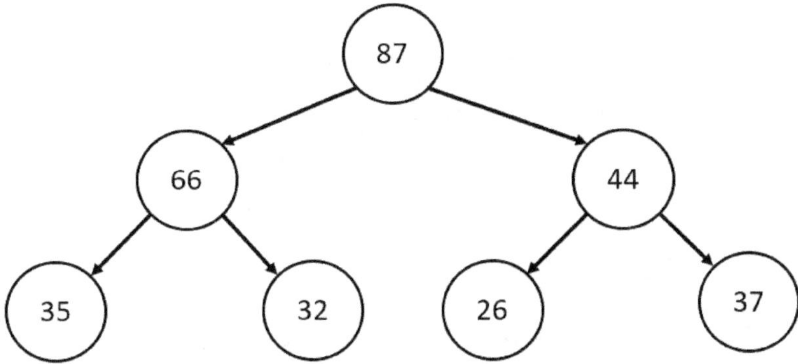

Figure 4.3: Example of a max heap

ing if a given value is the maximum value of an unsorted list. This task would be $\mathcal{O}(n)$ complexity, because you would be required to either determine the maximum value of the list or compare the input to every value in the list. With max heaps, we can determine if a value is the maximum in $\mathcal{O}(1)$ time by simply comparing it to the root node. Additionally, if we insert this value into the heap with an $\mathcal{O}(\log(n))$ operation, the heap is then in an appropriate state to perform the same check on a new value.

The next fundamental operation we can perform on a max heap is extracting the maximum value. The maximum value is always the root node, so finding the it is easy. The only complexity involved here is re-establishing the heap property after removing the root. See Figure 4.5 for a visualization of the process of removing 99 from the end-result of Figure 4.4.

Extracting the root node from the heap involves replacing it with the right-most bottom-most leaf node, then moving down tree, incrementally re-establishing the heap property. The heap itself has no concept of left-to-right ordering, so you can actually use any leaf node. As long as you keep moving the greatest value upward in the tree by swapping it with the temporary replacement node, you will re-establish the heap property. This process is also $\mathcal{O}(\log(n))$.

Heap extraction has many potentially useful properties. For example, say you wanted to extract the top $k = 5$ values of from a list of numbers. If that list of numbers is already organized in a heap, then that process would occur in $\mathcal{O}(k \log(n))$ time, which is faster than sorting the entire list. We will explore and profile this concept

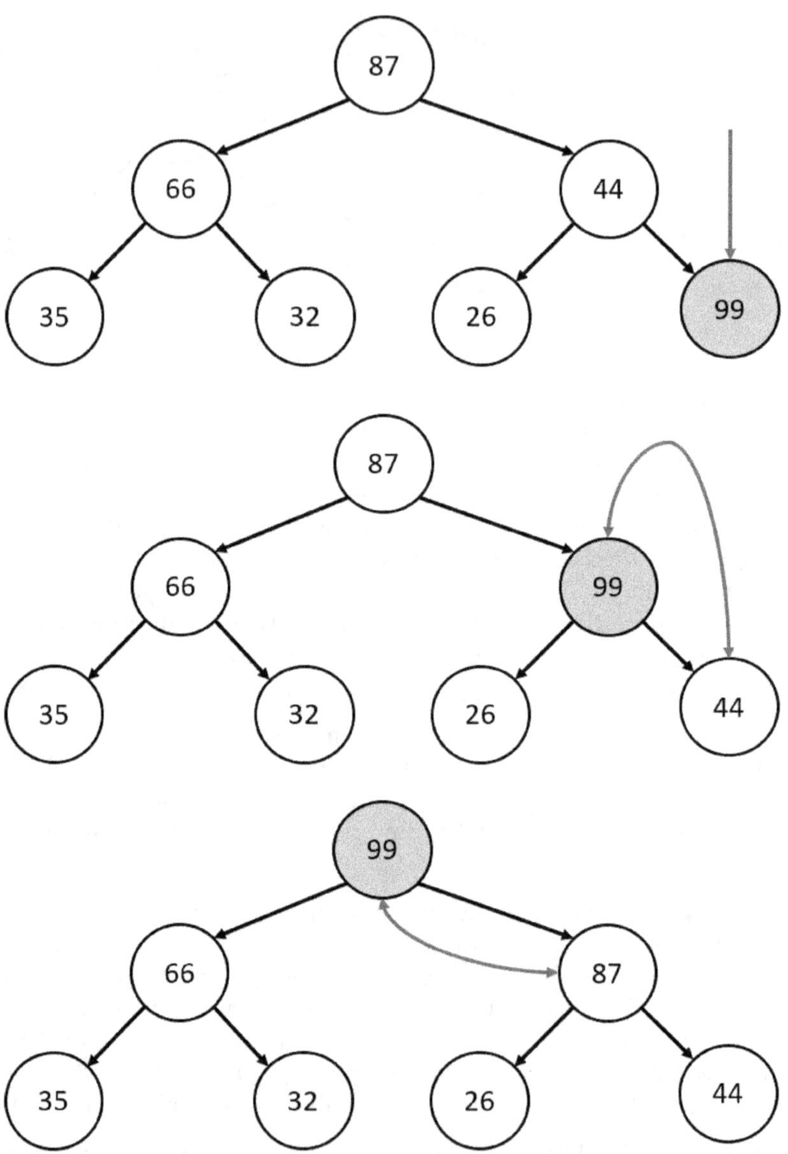

Figure 4.4: Inserting 99 into the max heap

further later in this chapter.

It is important to note that constructing a heap or converting a list of values into a heap is an $\mathcal{O}(n)$ operation. Constructing a heap involves performing a heap insert operation on every value in a list, which may lead us to believe the process is $\mathcal{O}(n \log(n))$. Nonetheless, it can be proven that the number of comparisons required to do it is not $n \log(n)$ but $2n$, making heap construction a $\mathcal{O}(n)$ algorithm.

Max heaps also have a min heap variant that works in the exact opposite way. The root node of a min heap is always the minimum node, and all parents are less than their children.

4.1.3 Binary Search Trees

A binary search tree is a configuration of a binary tree. On a binary search tree, every member of a left branch of a node is less than it, and every member of a right branch of a node is greater than it. The tree is constructed in this way to facilitate easy searches and lookups. See Figure 4.6 for an example.

It is very easy to imagine how these trees allow for easy searching. For example, if I wanted to figure out if the value 67 was in the tree, I would start at the root of 44, go right to 66, then go right again to 71. Since 71 is a leaf node, I can be certain that the value 67 is not in the tree, because I know that all values greater than 66 should live on the right branch of the 66 node. This search is $\mathcal{O}(\log(n))$ for n total nodes in the tree.

In a similar fashion to heaps, inserting and deleting elements from the tree are also $\mathcal{O}(\log(n))$ operations. It simply involves swapping elements around to meet the requirements of a binary search tree.

We will note again here than a binary search tree can be represented by a variety of data structures, and some of the most useful algorithms will construct and maintain them in very creative ways.

Now that we have laid the groundwork, we can start flying through sorting algorithms and profiling novel use cases. We will start with the task of sorting lists of numbers, and move on to some more creative applications of heaps and binary search trees.

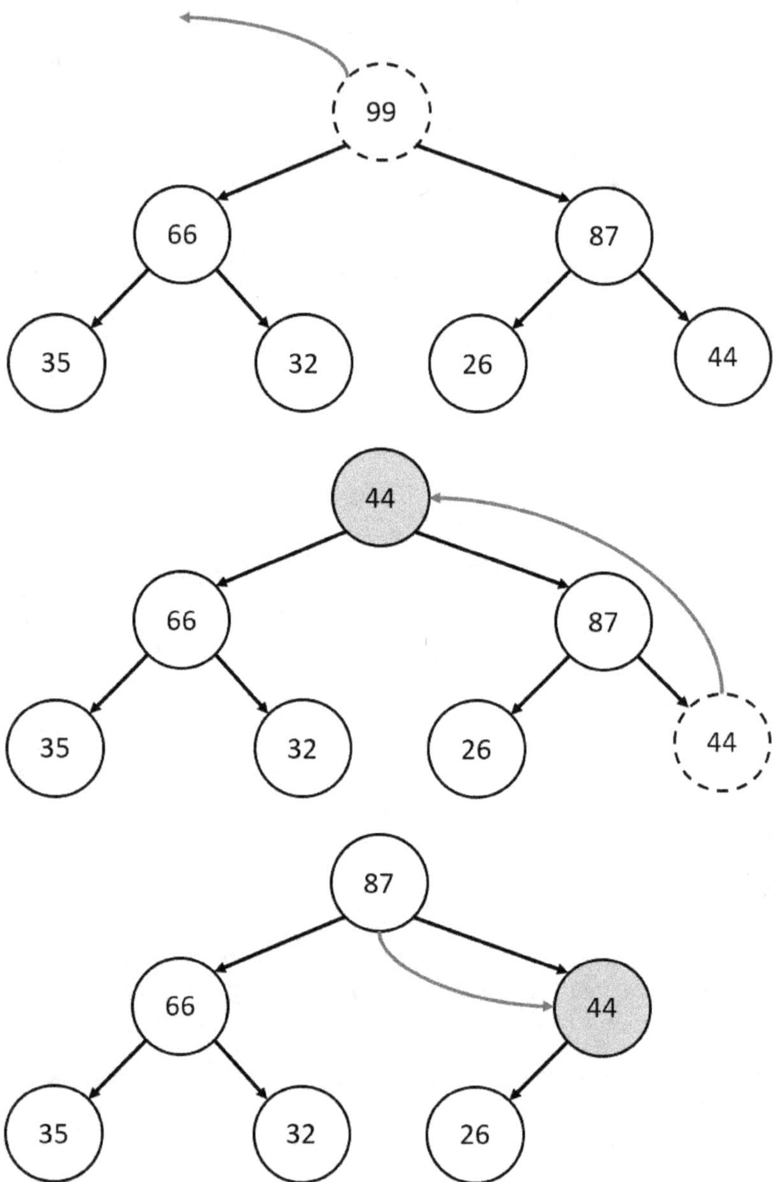

Figure 4.5: Extracting 99 from the max heap

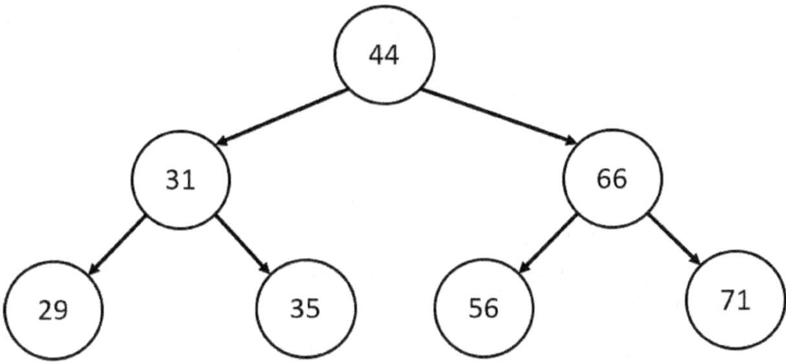

Figure 4.6: Binary search tree example

4.2 Sorting Lists

This is going to be a long section. Sorting algorithms are explained in nearly every algorithms textbook, and there are a lot of them. Further, sorting algorithms are notoriously hard to understand and reproduce from memory. Most of the good ones involve esoteric data structures and mind-bending recursions.

Lots of different and animated graphics and visualizations exist online to try to give programmers a more intuitive understanding of what actually happens in these algorithms. I believe the best way to learn them is write the algorithms out by hand, and run them over and over again, littering your own print statements throughout. Therefore, this section will not contain loquacious explanations of all the most common sorting algorithms. Rather, it will contain well-commented code and profiles of them. It will be up to each and every reader to spend sufficient time with them to develop an intuitive understanding of what they do, if he or she desires to understand them at all.

Note that we will always default to sorting lists in ascending order in this chapter.

4.2.1 Bubble Sort

Bubble sort is a simple $\mathcal{O}(n^2)$ in-place sorting algorithm. When we talk about sorting algorithms, or any algorithms for that matter, the term *in-place* means that we modify the input directly. We will often still return the list, but the list itself is being modified both inside and outside of the function.

Bubble sort works by iterating through the list as many times as needed, which it will need to do a maximum of n times. Inside the inner loop, bubble sort swaps adjacent values that are considered out of order. The algorithm gets its name because the larger values in the list appear to slowly *bubble* upwards in the same way an air bubble would escape a fish tank.

```python
def bubble_sort(values: List[float]) -> List[float]:
    """
    Bubble sorting is O(n^2) complexity and modifies the
    list in-place
    """

    n = len(values)

    # Set to true so that loop happens at least once
    swap_occurred = True
    while swap_occurred:

        # Consider finished if no swaps happen
        swap_occurred = False
        for i in range(n-1):

            # If something is out of order ...
            if values[i] > values[i+1]:

                # Swap the values
                values[i], values[i+1] = \
                    values[i+1], values[i]

                # Mark that we are unfinished because
                # we swapped something
                swap_occurred = True

    # Return a reference to the list
    return values
```

Listing 4.3: Bubble sort

The algorithm is $\mathcal{O}(n^2)$ complexity because the inner loop can only "bubble up" one element at a time into its correct position. For example, if we have a list [7,3,0,0,0,0,0], and we printed the output after every swap operation, we would get the following. First, the inner loop bubbles up the number 7 to the correct position, then it restarts and bubbles up 3 to the correct position.

```
# Initial list
[7, 3, 0, 0, 0, 0, 0]

# First while loop, 6 swaps
[3, 7, 0, 0, 0, 0, 0]
[3, 0, 7, 0, 0, 0, 0]
[3, 0, 0, 7, 0, 0, 0]
[3, 0, 0, 0, 7, 0, 0]
[3, 0, 0, 0, 0, 7, 0]
[3, 0, 0, 0, 0, 0, 7]

# Second while loop, 5 swaps
[0, 3, 0, 0, 0, 0, 7]
[0, 0, 3, 0, 0, 0, 7]
[0, 0, 0, 3, 0, 0, 7]
[0, 0, 0, 0, 3, 0, 7]
[0, 0, 0, 0, 0, 3, 7]
```

If we were to input a perfectly backwards list, [n, n-1, ..., 2, 1], the number of swap operations required would be as follows.

$$n + (n - 1) + \ldots + 2 + 1 =$$

$$\frac{n(n - 1)}{2} = \frac{n^2 - n}{2} = \mathcal{O}(n^2)$$

This simple example proves that the worst-case complexity of bubble sort is $\mathcal{O}(n^2)$. Additional probabilistic proofs can be done to prove that the complexity of performing bubble sort on a randomly ordered list of values is also $\mathcal{O}(n^2)$, indicating the average-case complexity is the same. We will further verify this in our profiling.

4.2.2   Selection Sort

Selection sort is another $\mathcal{O}(n^2)$ in-place sorting algorithm. The inner loop essentially runs an **argmin** function on a subset of the

list, and makes swaps in such a way that the final result is fully
sorted.

```python
def selection_sort(values: List[float]) -> List[float]:
    """
    Selection sort is O(n~2) complexity and modifies the
    list in-place
    """
    n = len(values)

    # Prepare to swap i with the lowest value above it
    for i in range(n):

        # Set i as the defeault value of the swap target
        min_idx = i

        # Loop through elements above i
        for j in range(i+1, n):

            # If anything is less than j, prepare to put
            # it in the i-th position
            if values[j] < values[min_idx]:
                min_idx = j

        # Make the swap
        values[i], values[min_idx] = \
            values[min_idx], values[i]

    # Return a reference to the list
    return values
```

Listing 4.4: Selection sort

If we were to input a perfectly backwards list like the following into
selection sort and print the values every time a swap is made, you
would get the following.

```python
# Initial values
[5, 4, 3, 2, 1]

# Loops for i in 0 through 4
[1, 4, 3, 2, 5]
[1, 2, 3, 4, 5]
[1, 2, 3, 4, 5]
```

```
[1, 2, 3, 4, 5]
[1, 2, 3, 4, 5]
```

Note how nothing happens to the list in the last 3 iterations of the loop. The list [5,4,3,2,1] only needs two swap operations in order to completely order it, those swaps being (1,5) and (2,4). The selection sort algorithm picks up on this and makes the appropriate swaps. While it might seem wasteful that the outer loop is run an additional three times after the list is fully sorted, note that the last few inner loops work with a progressively smaller slice of the overall list. In other words, it is not that wasteful for there to be no work done in the last few inner loops. It would probably be more wasteful to manually check that the whole list is sorted, in the sense that it would require more comparisons that the alternative.

In the last subsection we proved that the worst-case complexity of bubble sort was $\mathcal{O}(n^2)$ by proving that the number of comparisons and swaps made was $n + (n - 1) + ... + 1$ on a backward-sorted list. This same argument follows for the best, average, and worst case for selection sort. The number of iterations of the loop and the number of comparisons are fixed at $n + (n - 1) + ... + 1$ for selection sort regardless of the sortedness of the input list. Selection sort gets some of its empirical speed advantages over other sorting algorithms because the number of swap operations is fixed at n.

4.2.3 Insertion Sort

Insertion sort is yet another $\mathcal{O}(n^2)$ sorting algorithm. It is interesting because it happens to be very fast on small lists of values, and is used in some special cases in standard sorting functions of various languages. We will talk about how and when selection sort is used later in this section. For now, see Listing 4.5 for the algorithm.

```python
def insertion_sort(values: List[float]) -> List[float]:
    """
    Insertion sort is O(n^2) complexity and modifies the
    list in-place
    """

    n = len(values)

    # Prepare to insert the i-th element in the appropriate
    # place, over and over
    for i in range(1, n):
```

```python
        # Keep track of initial i-th value because it might
        # get overwritten
        value_to_insert = values[i]

        # Descend j-1 to 0 looking for a home for i
        j = i-1
        while j >= 0 and values[j] > value_to_insert:

            # Shift the larger values up along the way
            values[j+1] = values[j]

            # Descend further
            j -= 1

        # Insert the i-th value in the right place
        if i != j+1:
            values[j+1] = value_to_insert

    # Return a reference to the list
    return values
```

Listing 4.5: Insertion sort

The best way to explain insertion sort is to look at how it treats
a backwards-sorted list. For every i in the outer loop, it fully
sorts the list values[:i] by inserting the new values[i] into the
appropriate place in the list, shifting all of the larger values upwards
to fit it.

```python
# Initial value
[5, 4, 3, 2, 1]

# Outer loops 1 through 4
[4, 5, 3, 2, 1]
[3, 4, 5, 2, 1]
[2, 3, 4, 5, 1]
[1, 2, 3, 4, 5]
```

Due to the structure of the inner while loop of this algorithm,
it actually has a best case performance of $\mathcal{O}(n)$, meaning it will
not perform unnecessary swaps or comparisons if the input list is
already sorted. The same cannot be said for the selection sort
algorithm.

4.2.4 Heap Sort

We discussed earlier in this chapter how heaps work, and we noted the various complexities of performing certain operations on heaps. This subsection will bring all of those concepts together to build the heap sort algorithm, which is $\mathcal{O}(n\log(n))$.

We also discussed earlier in this chapter how a heap is a form of a tree, and trees themselves can be represented as numerous different data structures. The heap sort algorithm will represent the heap as a list, where the children of a node i are located at indexes 2*i+1 and 2*i+2 of the list. In other words, a list representing a heap would have to pass the test in Listing 4.6.

```python
def assert_is_heaped(values: List[float]):
    """
    Checks that the values of a list satisfy the max-heap
    conditions where the children of element i are located
    at 2*i+1 and 2*i+2.
    """

    n = len(values)
    msg = 'Did not satisfy heap condition.'
    for i in range(n):
        l = 2 * i + 1
        r = 2 * i + 2

        if l < n:
            assert values[i] >= values[l], msg

        if r < n:
            assert values[i] >= values[r], msg
```

Listing 4.6: Check that a list is heaped

In order to build the max heap, we will introduce the function `_heapify`, which will serve multiple purposes in the heap sort. See Listing 4.7 for the routine to build the max heap. Recall that the process of building a max heap is $\mathcal{O}(n)$.

```python
def _heapify(values: List[float], heap_size: int,
        root_node: int):
    """
    The ubiquitous heapify function that handles both heap
    construction and root extraction on a list-based heap,
```

```python
    where the children of element i are located at
    2*i+1 and 2*i+2.
    """

    n = heap_size

    # Index of the root
    i = root_node

    # Default index of the largest value
    j = root_node

    # Probe these elements as potential roots
    l = 2 * i + 1 # Index of left child node
    r = 2 * i + 2 # Index of right child node

    # Set j to the largest value of a child
    if l < n and values[l] > values[i]:
        j = l

    if r < n and values[r] > values[j]:
        j = r

    # If the root is not the max, set a new root and send
    # it back through
    if j != i:
        # Swap max and root elements
        values[i], values[j] = values[j], values[i]

        # Recurse
        _heapify(values, n, j)


def build_max_heap(values: List[float]) -> List[float]:
    """
    Converts values into a max heap.
    """

    n = len(values)

    # Create a max-heap from values
    for i in range(n, -1, -1):
        _heapify(values, n, i)
```

```python
    # Return a reference to values
    return values
```

Listing 4.7: Build max heap

If you pass the output list `values` through the function `build_max_heap`, it should have no problem passing the tests defined in `assert_is_heaped`.

Building the heap is the hard part. Now that we have a heap, we can iteratively pull the root node out, store it somewhere else in the list, then shrink and re-heapify the remaining values. The resulting heap keeps shrinking until all that is left is a list of sorted values. See Listing 4.8 for the full heap sort function.

```python
def heap_sort(values: List[float]) -> List[float]:
    """
    Heap sort converts values to a list-based heap, then
    extracts the root iteratively until it has achieved a
    sorted list.

    O(n*log(n)) complexity
    """
    n = len(values)

    values = build_max_heap(values)

    # Successively move the root node to the top
    for i in range(n-1, 0, -1):

        # Store the current root node as i
        values[i], values[0] = values[0], values[i]

        # Heapify the remaining values
        _heapify(values, i, 0)

    return values
```

Listing 4.8: Heap sort

The inner workings of this algorithm are harder to visualize, because the algorithm itself is recursive. If we print the list of values after each call to `_heapify` in the loop, we can get a good idea of what is going on.

```
# Initial values
[7, 6, 5, 4, 3, 2, 1]

# Heapified values
[7, 6, 5, 4, 3, 2, 1]

# 0 through 5 are a heap, 6 is sorted
[6, 4, 5, 1, 3, 2, 7]

# 0 through 4 are a heap, 5 through 6 are sorted
[5, 4, 2, 1, 3, 6, 7]

# 0 through 3 are a heap, 4 through 6 are sorted
[4, 3, 2, 1, 5, 6, 7]

# 0 through 2 are a heap, 3 through 6 are sorted
[3, 1, 2, 4, 5, 6, 7]

# 0 through 1 are a heap, 2 through 6 are sorted
[2, 1, 3, 4, 5, 6, 7]

# 0 is a heap, 1 through 6 are sorted
# Final result is sorted
[1, 2, 3, 4, 5, 6, 7]
```

We will move on to discuss merge sort and quicksort, neither of
which rely on an elegant underlying data structure like a heap.
Rather, the following algorithms rely on beautiful acts of recursion.

4.2.5   Merge Sort

Merge sort is an $\mathcal{O}(n \log(n))$ algorithm that relies on recursion and
ordered pairs. As with most recursive algorithms, I believe the
best way to understand it is to write it out by hand using your
own variable names and adding you own comments. It is difficult
to effectively visualize what is going on in this algorithm, because
the depth of recursion gives the appearance that many things are
happening simultaneously.

```
def _merge(left: List[float],
    right: List[float]) -> List[float]:
        """
```

```python
    Merging part of the merge_sort algorithm.
    """
    # Output
    _sorted = []

    # Left and right indexes
    l = r = 0

    # Left and right lengths
    n_left, n_right = len(left), len(right)

    # We incremenet either l or r every time, so it should
    # take this n_left + n_right total steps to reach the
    # end of each
    for _ in range(n_left + n_right):

        # We are still working through both right and left
        if l < n_left and r < n_right:

            # Add the smallest element and increment
            if left[l] <= right[r]:
                _sorted.append(left[l])
                l += 1
            else:
                _sorted.append(right[r])
                r += 1

        # We are at the end of the left list, add rights
        elif l == n_left:
            _sorted.append(right[r])
            r += 1

        # We are at the end of the right list, add lefts
        elif r == n_right:
            _sorted.append(left[l])
            l += 1

    return _sorted


def merge_sort(values: List[float]) -> List[float]:
    """
```

```python
    Sequentially split lists into ordered pairs, then merges
    the results
    """
    n = len(values)

    # Exit early on n == 1, when all possible splits have
    # been done
    if n == 1:
        return values

    # Index of integer midpoint
    i_mid = len(values) // 2

    left: List[float] = merge_sort(values[:i_mid])
    right: List[float] = merge_sort(values[i_mid:])

    return _merge(left, right)
```

Listing 4.9: Merge sort

It is worth noting that this algorithm can be generalized to work on lists of any size, and its intermediate results can be saved and reused. Due to this property, an extension of merge sort is typically used whenever the list of values is so large that it cannot be fit into memory. The merge sorts can be performed on many smaller individual files before the final result is merged into a single larger file in a process called *external merge sort*.

4.2.6   Quick Sort

Quick sort is an $\mathcal{O}(n \log(n))$ algorithm that relies on recursively ordering elements of a list around a pivot point. As with the previous algorithm, the best way to attempt to understand it is to write out the code yourself with your own variable names and comments.

```python
def _partition(values: List[float], l: int, r: int):
    """
    Move l and r inward, swapping where appropriate. Return
    the crossover index as a partition value for future
    recursions of the function
    """

    # Grab some middle value as the pivot
```

```python
    # Index can be a random integer in (l,r) or a midpoint
    pivot = values[(l + r) // 2]

    # Make appropriate swaps until l and r cross over
    while l <= r:

        # Find an element on the left that should be on the
        # right
        while values[l] < pivot:
            l += 1

        # Find an element on the right that should be on
        # the left
        while values[r] > pivot:
            r -= 1

        # If l and r did not cross over, make a swap
        if l <= r:
            values[l], values[r] = values[r], values[l]
            l += 1
            r -= 1

    return l

def _quick_sort(values: List[float], l: int, r: int):
    """
    Sorts values in-place by recursively swapping values
    around a pivot point

    l is a 'lefthand' index and r is a 'righthand' per the
    algorithm
    """
    i = _partition(values, l, r)
    if l < i - 1:
        _quick_sort(values, l, i-1)
    if i < r:
        _quick_sort(values, i, r)

def quick_sort(values: List[float]):
    """
    Wrapper around the main quick_sort logic
    """
```

```
n = len(values)
_quick_sort(values, 0, n-1)
```

Listing 4.10: Quick sort

Quick sort can also be extended to work with intermediate parts of massive data that cannot fit into memory. The quicksort-like algorithms that work with out-of-memory data are known as distribution sorting algorithms.

4.2.7   Timsort

Timsort is the default sorting algorithm used in a number of platforms and languages including Python, Java, and Swift. Timsort was first developed by Tim Peters in 2002 specifically for use in Python. Timsort, unlike the aforementioned algorithms, is all about minimizing execution time on real-world data, and it attempts takes advantage of every such opportunity to do so.

Timsort is the most common algorithm in a class known as adaptive sorting algorithms. Adaptive sorting algorithms, in general, combine numerous sorting algorithms or sorting concepts with the goal of minimizing computation time. These adaptive sorting algorithms are not neatly defined mathematical concepts that can be expressed as pseudo-code. Rather, they are highly optimized low-level algorithms that often span hundreds or thousands of lines of C code. For Timsort, that translates to an algorithm that does the following.

1. Look for existing sections or *runs* of already sorted data. These are surprisingly common in real-world data.
2. Use merge sort where appropriate to combine pre-existing runs with unsorted sections of data.
3. Use insertion sort on small data sets or small sections of data wherever it will likely provide a speed-up.

This is definitely an over-simplification of Timsort. Readers are encouraged to investigate the Python source code to develop an understanding of Timsort if they so desire. We will move on to simply profile it against the other algorithms we discussed here.

```
def python_native_sort(values: List[float]):
    values.sort()
```

Listing 4.11: Native Python sort (Timsort)

Timsort is $\mathcal{O}(n\log(n))$ in the worst case and $\mathcal{O}(n)$ if the list if already sorted. As a final point about adaptive sorting algorithms, it is worthwhile to note that any sorting algorithm with poor best-case complexity can be improved by wrapping it in the following function.

```python
def improved_best_case_wrapper(values: List[float],
    sorting_algo: Callable[[List], List]) -> List[float]:
    """
    Wrap any sorting algorithm with this in order to convert
    its best-case complexity to O(n)
    """
    n = len(values)

    # Check if it is sorted
    is_sorted = all(
        values[i] <= values[i+1] for i in range(n-1)
    )

    # Just return if sorted
    if is_sorted:
        return values

    # Fall back on the real sorting algo
    return sorting_algo(values)

values = improved_best_case_wrapper(values, insertion_sort)
```

Listing 4.12: Improved best case wrapper

4.2.8 Performance and Conclusions

The profiles in Figures 4.7 and 4.8 show clearly that Timsort outperforms the competitors, even on random data, for which is was not specifically designed. It is worth noting that Timsort is highly optimized at the C level, which certainly contributes to its significant outperformance of the other algorithms.

f	n	t (ms)	n/t
bubble_sort	1E+04	1.4E+04	7.3E-01
selection_sort	1E+04	4.2E+03	2.4E+00
insertion_sort	1E+04	4.1E+03	2.4E+00

f	n	t (ms)	n/t
heap_sort	1E+06	1.2E+04	8.7E+01
merge_sort_timeable	1E+06	5.7E+03	1.8E+02
quick_sort	1E+06	3.8E+03	2.6E+02
python_native_sort	1E+06	7.2E+02	1.4E+03

Table 4.1: Sorting algorithm performance

Ultimately, this comparison of sorting algorithm efficiency is a little bit unfair because Python's native sorting algorithm is the only one optimized with low-level code. The next section will fly through various sorting algorithms in **numpy** and **pandas** to compare their performance when they are all optimized at the C-level.

4.3   Optimized Sorting Algorithms

This section will compare the performance of quick sort, heap sort, and Timsort using optimized **numpy** routines in order to get an apples-to-apples comparison of sorting algorithm performance. The **pandas** variants of these algorithms directly call the underlying **numpy** routines, so we will not explore them.

```python
def python_timsort(values: List[float]):
    values.sort()


def numpy_timsort(values: List[float]):
    return np.sort(values, kind='stable')


def numpy_quicksort(values: List[float]):
    return np.sort(values, kind='quicksort')


def numpy_heapsort(values: List[float]):
    return np.sort(values, kind='heapsort')
```

Listing 4.13: Optimized sorting algorithms

Keep in mind which plots use random data and which plots use natural data. The Timsort algorithm is optimized to perform best on datasets that have a high number of already-sorted segments, which is considered to be typical in real-world data.

Figure 4.7: Input to our natural dataset

Our natural dataset in these profiles is the pixels of a contour plot taken from the `matplotlib` documentation converted into a one-dimensional array. See Figure 4.7 for the image used to construct our so-called natural dataset. Regardless of whether this data is indicative of what a natural data set looks like, Timsort is able to take advantages of its large number of already-sorted segments to achieve the best performance.

f	n	t (ms)	n/t
python_timsort	1E+07	9.9E+03	1.0E+03
numpy_timsort	1E+07	2.0E+03	4.9E+03
numpy_quicksort	1E+07	1.8E+03	5.6E+03
numpy_heapsort	1E+07	3.3E+03	3.0E+03

Table 4.2: Optimized sorting algorithms on random data

f	n	t (ms)	n/t
python_timsort	1E+07	2.0E+02	4.9E+04
numpy_timsort	1E+07	2.3E+01	4.3E+05
numpy_quicksort	1E+07	2.1E+02	4.8E+04
numpy_heapsort	1E+07	5.6E+02	1.8E+04

Table 4.3: Optimized sorting algorithms on natural data

4.4   Partial Sorting Algorithms

The whole point of exploring heap sort was to uncover a better solution to the following problem. Given a list of n values, find the top k values.

We have discussed already how establishing a heap is $\mathcal{O}(n)$ and extracting the root node from a heap is $\mathcal{O}(\log(n))$. Given these facts, the process of finding the top k elements of a list of length n should be $\mathcal{O}(n + k\log(n))$. Recall that the complexity for the best-known algorithms for sorting an entire list is $\mathcal{O}(n\log(n))$. So, when we only seek the top k elements, we should be able to use heap sort to outperform a complete sort for large n. This section will test that hypothesis, and show when and where it is actually practical to substitute a full sort for a heap sort.

See Listing 4.14 for a method of finding the top k values. This algorithm sorts the entire list in-place using Python's native `.sort()`, then returns the first k values. We know by now that this algorithm is $\mathcal{O}(n\log(n))$, because that is the complexity of the sorting step.

```python
def naive_find_top_k(values: List[float],
    k: int=20) -> List[float]:
    """

    Given a list of values, find the highest k values by
    sorting the entire list first. This is O(n*log(n))
    """

    values.sort(reverse=True)
    return values[:k]
```

Listing 4.14: Naive find top k values

See Listing 4.15 for a method of finding the top k values using Python's `heapq` library. The `heapq` library is part of the Python standard library and provides a number of optimized interfaces for managing heaps as Python lists. The way that `heapq` manages heaps is actually the same novel way that the heapsort algorithm does, where the children of `i` live at `2*i+1` and `2*i+2`.

Running `heapq.nlargest` on a vanilla Python list both converts it into a heap and performs sequential root node extraction `k` times, providing us with a one-line solution to our problem. To understand how this works on a deeper level, see the section on heaps and heap sorting earlier in this chapter.

Since establishing a heap is an $\mathcal{O}(n)$ operation and extracting the root node is a $\mathcal{O}(\log(n))$ operation, we know that this algorithm runs in $\mathcal{O}(n + k\log(n))$ time.

```python
import heapq

def heap_find_top_k(values: List[float],
    k: int=20) -> List[float]:
    """
    Given a list of values, convert it into a heap in-place,
    then extract the top k values from the heap. This is
    O(n + k*log(n))
    """

    return heapq.nlargest(k, values)
```

Listing 4:15: Heap find top k values

For sake of completeness, we will show how to accomplish the same procedure defined in Listing 4.15 using lower-level features of Python's **heapq** module. See Listing 4.16 for a more verbose way to accomplish the above. Python's **heapq** library only support min heaps, so we first establish a min heap using the negative of the elements of **values**. Then, we perform heap extraction while converting the negative values back to positive values. The result is the same as in Listing 4.15, but it is considerably slower, presumably because we are circumventing low-level optimizations used by **heapq.nlargest**.

```python
import heapq

def heap_find_top_k_expanded(values: List[float],
    k: int=20) -> List[float]:
    """
    Given a list of values, convert it into a heap in-place,
    then extract the  top k values from the heap. This is
    O(n + k*log(n))
    """

    _heap: List[float] = []
    for v in values:
        heapq.heappush(_heap, -v)

    top_k: List[float] = []
```

```
    for i in range(k):
        top_k.append(-heapq.heappop(_heap))

    return top_k
```

Listing 4.16: Heap find top k values (expanded)

See Figures 4.14 and 4.15 for the performance of various top-k algorithms. Both variants of the heap sort algorithm handily outperform vanilla sorting for medium and large n.

f	n	t (ms)	n/t
naive_find_top_k	1E+07	1.0E+04	9.8E+02
heap_find_top_k	1E+07	3.7E+02	2.7E+04
heap_find_top_k_expanded	1E+07	3.0E+03	3.3E+03

Table 4.4: Partial sorting algorithms with heaps

4.5   Binary Search Algorithms

Binary searches involve finding an element inside an already-sorted list. When a list is sorted in advance, we can treat the list like a binary search tree where the middle element is the root node, and the middle elements of the right and left halves of the list are the child nodes, and so on, recursively. We will compare the performance of basic searching to binary searching, then take a look at Python's `bisect` module that comes with the standard library.

See Listing 4.17 for an `in`-like operator with early stopping, for sake of comparison. Note that this algorithm assumes nothing about the already-sorted nature of the list.

```
def naive_in_operator(values: List[float],
    target: float) -> bool:
    """

    Given a list of floats that are assumed to be sorted,
    determine if an element is in the list with early
    stopping. This is O(n)
    """

    for value in values:
        if target == value:
            return True
```

Listing 4:17: Naive in operator

Listing 4.18 shows a classic formulation of a binary search algorithm. Of all of the recursive algorithms we have discussed in this chapter, this is likely the easiest to understand. The recursive algorithm repeatedly chops the list in half until it has only one element. Then, it tests if that element is equal to the target element. If we place a print statement inside the recursive part of this algorithm, it is easily to verify that the number of times it recurses is roughly $\log_2(n)$ for n elements in the list.

It is important to note that this algorithm can also be used to return the index of the matching element, or the nearest index below the matching element. This index is commonly done in a lot of important software that utilizes binary searching.

Note that we specify the input values to be a **numpy** array in this algorithm. It is important that this algorithm passes references to the slices of **values** rather than copies of **values**. By default Python lists return copies of slices when indexed, but **numpy** arrays return references to the slices. If we do not slice by reference here, we lose nearly all of the speed benefits of binary searching. Alternate formulations of binary search algorithms exist that utilize boundary management as opposed to slices. These versions do not suffer from this problem, regardless of the input data type, but they suffer from poor readability and susceptibility to off-by-one errors.

```python
def _binary_search_in(values: np.ndarray,
    target: float) -> bool:
    """

    Recursive part of binary_search_in
    """


    # Split list in half
    n = len(values)
    i = n // 2

    if n > 1:
        # Search the upper or lower part of the list
        if target >= values[i]:
            return _binary_search_in(values[i:], target)
        else:
            return _binary_search_in(values[:i], target)
```

```python
    else:
        # Else, test for equality
        return values[i] == target


def binary_search_in(values: np.ndarray,
    target: float) -> bool:
    """

    Given a numpy array of floats that are assumed to be
    sorted, determine if an element is in it. We use numpy
    arrays here because it is important that array slices
    are passed by reference, rather than copied.
    This is O(log(n))
    """

    return _binary_search_in(values, target)
```

Listing 4.18: Binary search in

Python's **bisect** library provides optimized utilities for working with already-sorted lists using binary search algorithms. In Listing 4.19, we find the insertion point of **target** in **values**, then compare the target to the value of the insertion point if it is within the boundaries. The *insertion point* is simply the point at which you would insert **target** in **values** in order to maintain the sortedness of the list.

```python
def bisect_search_in(values: List[float],
    target: float) -> bool:
    """

    Given a list of floats that are assumed to be sorted,
    determine if an element is in the list using Python's
    bisect library. This is O(log(n))
    """


    # Find the insertion point of target within values to
    # maintain search order using binary search
    i = bisect.bisect_left(values, target)

    # If in bounds, make comparison
    if 0 <= i < len(values):
        return values[i] == target

    # Otherwise it is definitely not a match
    return False
```

Listing 4.19: Bisect search in

f	n	t (ms)	n/t
naive_in_operator	1E+07	1.4E+03	7.4E+03
binary_search_in	1E+07	1.8E-01	5.7E+07
bisect_search_in	1E+07	1.4E-02	7.0E+08

Table 4.5: Binary search

4.6 Conclusion

The discoveries discussed so far in this book can explain a great number of critical applications of computer science. For example, databases are able to look up arbitrary rows of data so quickly because they maintain multiple concurrent binary search trees. Heap sorting is used to help find the shortest path to a destination in GPS navigation. Adaptive searches take us beyond the limits of Big-O notation towards a probabilistic compute-time minimizing solution for general usage.

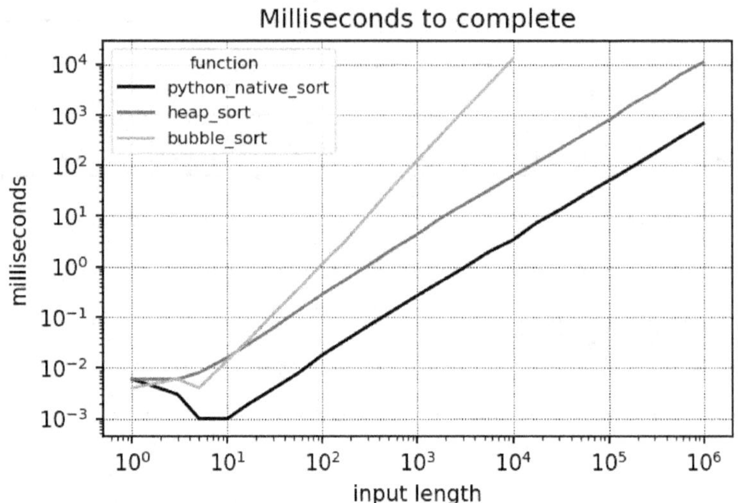

Figure 4.8: Sorting algorithm execution time (random data)

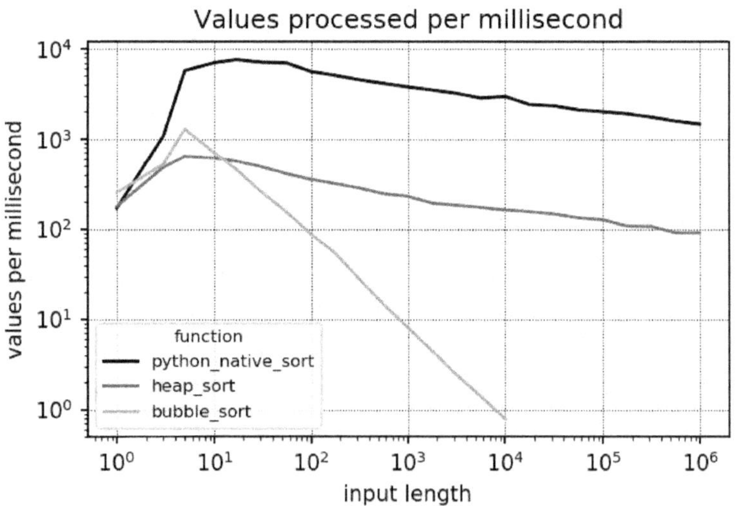

Figure 4.9: Sorting algorithm efficiency (random data)

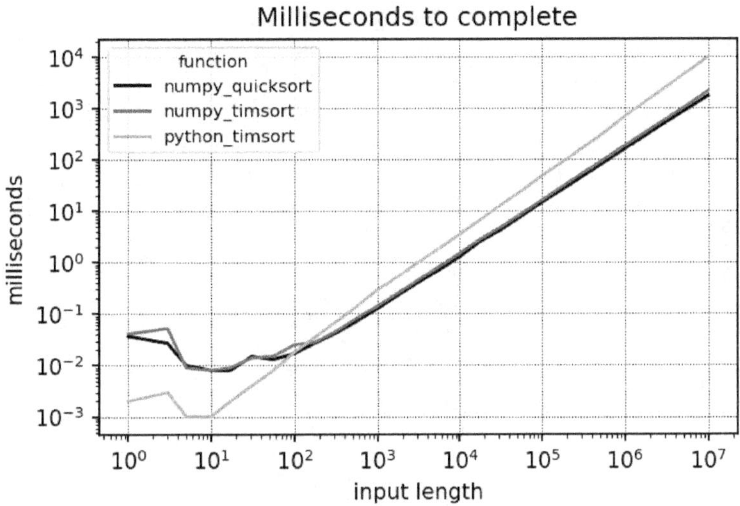

Figure 4.10: Optimized sorting execution time (random data)

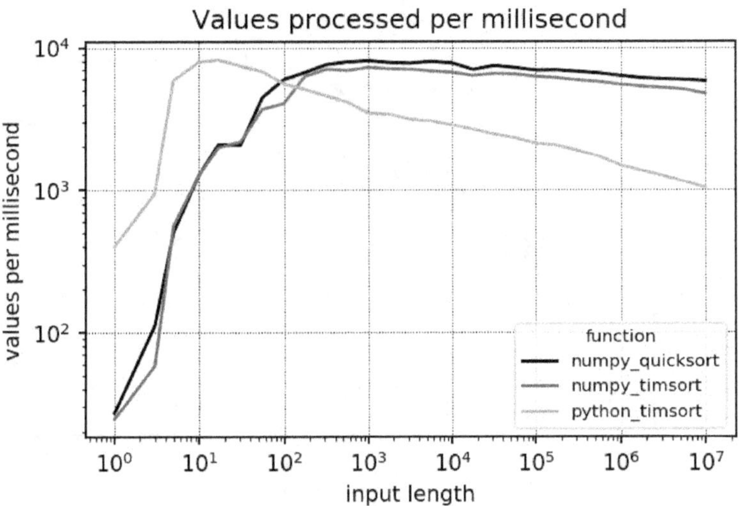

Figure 4.11: Optimized sorting efficiency (random data)

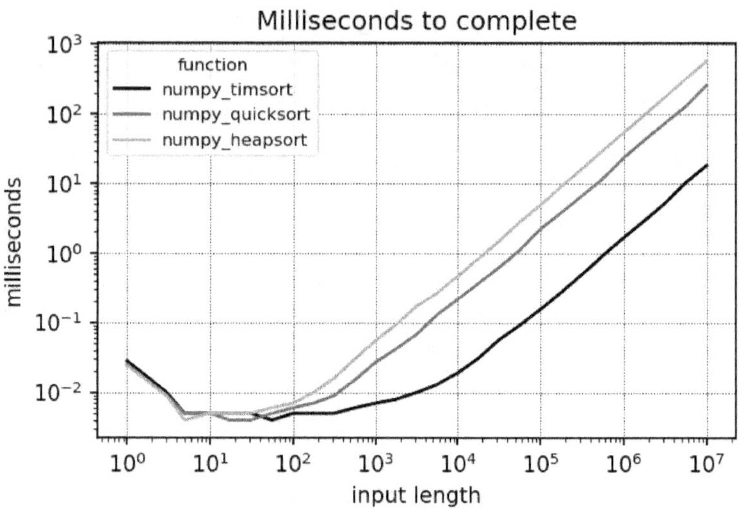

Figure 4.12: Optimized sorting execution time (natural data)

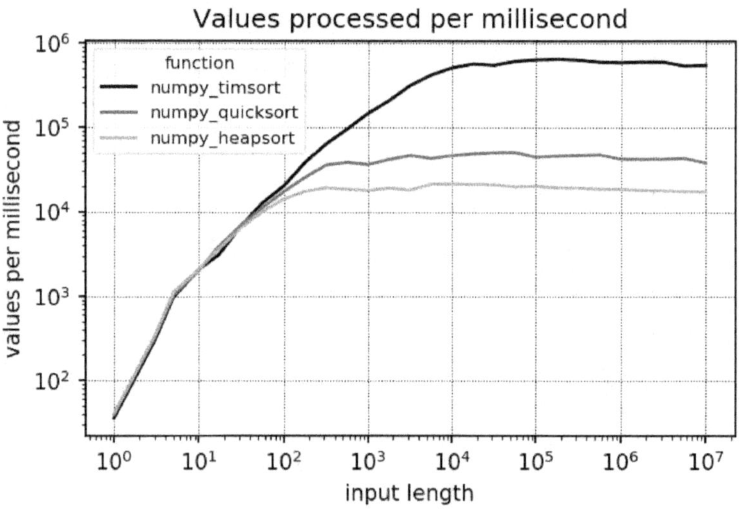

Figure 4.13: Optimized sorting efficiency (natural data)

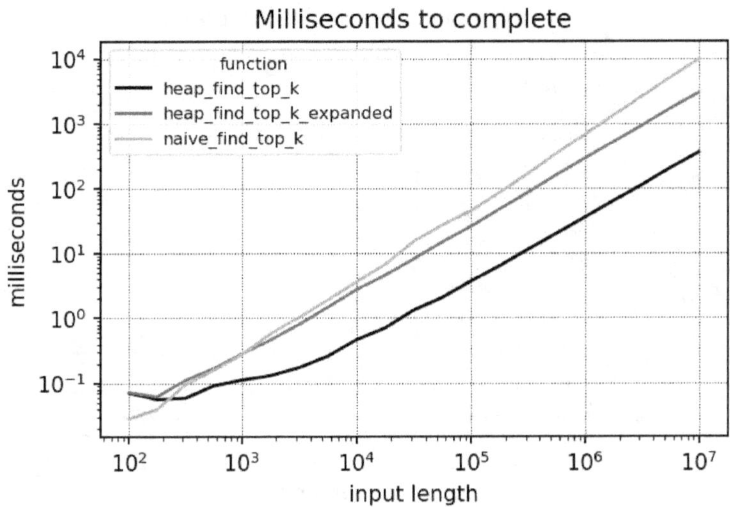

Figure 4.14: Partial sorting execution time

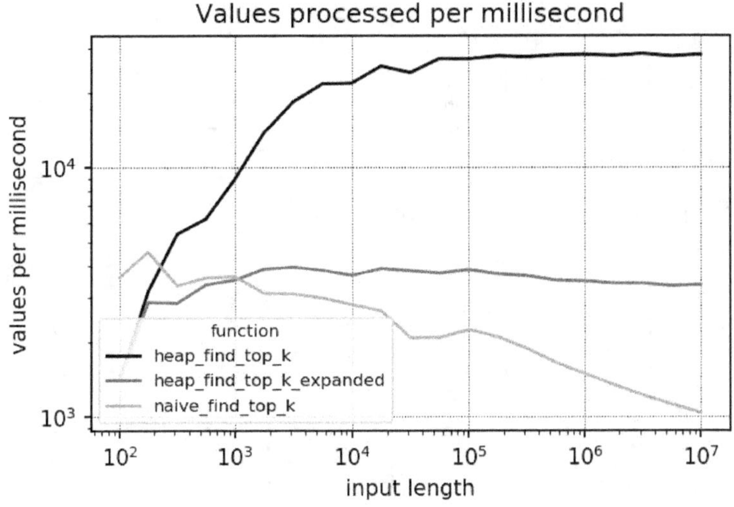

Figure 4.15: Partial sorting efficiency

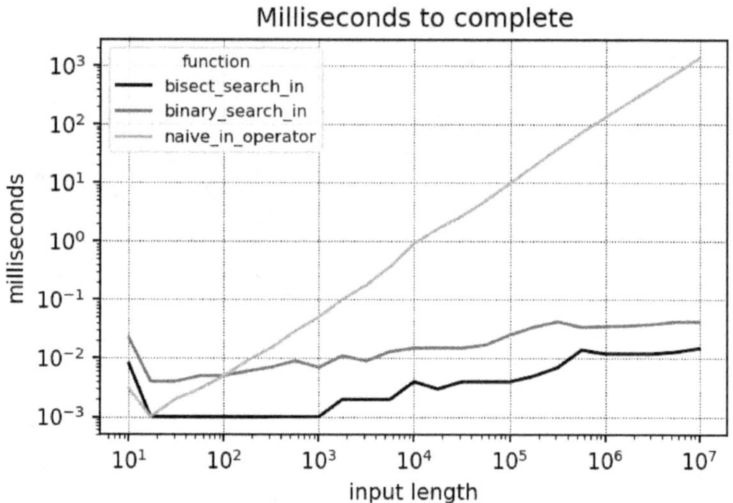

Figure 4.16: Binary search execution time

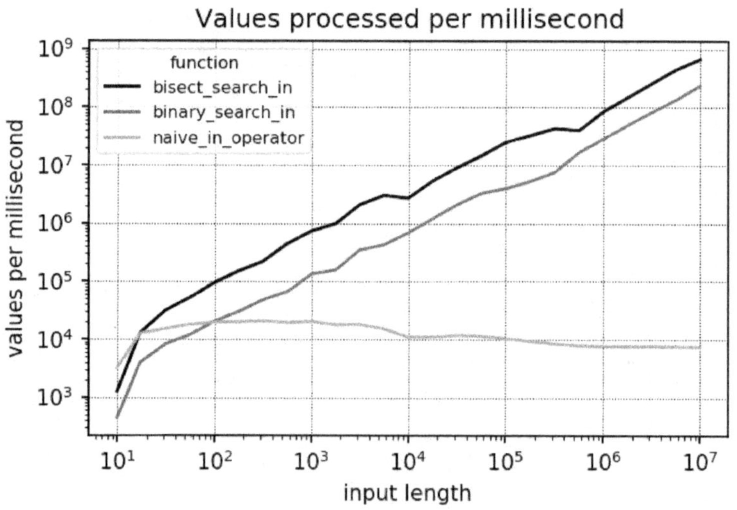

Figure 4.17: Binary search efficiency

Chapter 5

Declaring Things

So far in this book, we have optimized a lot of algorithms. While we have been focusing on time complexity, we have often handled memory complexity silently without giving much explanation as to how or why it improves compute time. This chapter will be all about memory complexity.

Memory allocation and data modification are expensive and insidious drags on performance. Just like time complexity, the sources of memory complexity can be hidden and hard to diagnose. In this chapter, we will discuss a number of ways of declaring and modifying various data structures while profiling their execution time. Throughout, we will find that allocating the least memory possible, after minimizing time complexity, is almost always the best solution. For readers, most of the utility of this chapter will be in revealing best-practices for declaring all sorts of data structures.

5.1 Declaring Strings

Strings are a really simple data structure, so we will start with them. Using the `sys.getsizeof` function, we can easily see how size in bytes of a string increases with its length.

```
import sys
import string
```

```python
for i in range(10):
    some_string = string.ascii_lowercase[:i]
    string_size = sys.getsizeof(some_string)
    print(f'{some_string:<10}{string_size:>4} bytes')

# Returns ...
#                 49 bytes
# a               50 bytes
# ab              51 bytes
# abc             52 bytes
# abcd            53 bytes
# abcde           54 bytes
# abcdef          55 bytes
# abcdefg         56 bytes
# abcdefgh        57 bytes
# abcdefghi       58 bytes
```

Listing 5.1: String size

Listing 5.1 shows us that the minimum size of a string is 49 bytes, and it grows by 1 byte for each character we add. It is worth noting here that all of these experiments will be run in an Anaconda environment using Python 3.7, and the exact number may differ based on your Python installation. Nonetheless, we see that even the smallest string incurs a significant amount of memory overhead when compared to a string of 10 times its length. This is the foundation for the following arguments about string manipulation and memory management.

```python
def slow_concatenate_words(the_words: List[str]) -> str:
    """
    Concatenate a list of strings. This has O(mn^2) memory
    complexity for n words with an average length of m.
    """

    result: str = ''
    for word in the_words:
        result += word
    return result
```

Listing 5.2: Slow concatenate string

```python
def fast_concatenate_words(the_words: List[str]) -> str:
    """
    Concatenate a list of strings. This has O(mn) memory
```

```
    complexity for n words with an average length of m.
    """
return ''.join(the_words)
```

Listing 5.3: Fast concatenate string

f	n	t (ms)	n/t
slow_concatenate_words	1E+07	6.1E+02	1.6E+04
fast_concatenate_words	1E+07	1.2E+02	8.1E+04

Table 5.1: String concatenation performance

5.2 Declaring Lists

In order to test the declaration speed of lists, we will attempt to flatten large lists of lists. By flattening, we mean converting a nested list into a simple list. For example, the list [[1,2], [3,4,5], [6]] would become [1,2,3,4,5,6]. Based on the results of our string experiments, we might think we know the outcome of these experiments, but they are not that simple. Lists are an elegant and ubiquitous data structure in Python that serve multiple core functions in computer science. As a result, they are optimized quite effectively and sometimes unintuitively.

```
def slow_add_flatten_lists(
    the_lists: List[List[str]]) -> List[str]:
    """
    Flatten a list of lists via list addition. This has
    O(mn^2) compexity for n lists with average length m
    """
    result: List[str] = []
    for _list in the_lists:
        result = result + _list
    return result
```

Listing 5.4: Slow flatten lists

Listing 5.4 flattens the list by iteratively reconstructing and reassigning the list to **result**. This is deliberately terrible memory management.

```python
def add_flatten_lists(
    the_lists: List[List[str]]) -> List[str]:
    """
    Flatten a list of lists via list addition
    """

    result: List[str] = []
    for _list in the_lists:
        result += _list
    return result
```

Listing 5.5: Add flatten lists

One would imagine that Listing 5.5 behaves the same way as Listing 5.4, because a += b is typically equivalent to a = a + b, but that is not the case. For some reason, Listing 5.5 performs better than Listing 5.4 and better than all alternatives presented in this section. Clearly, the += operator is optimized at some level for lists, but it is unclear why this operator is more optimized than some functions that do similar things, like .extend.

```python
def extend_flatten_lists(
    the_lists: List[List[str]]) -> List[str]:
    """
    Flatten a list of lists via extend
    """

    result: List[str] = []
    for _list in the_lists:
        result.extend(_list)
    return result
```

Listing 5.6: Extend flatten lists

Listing 5.6 uses list.extend to flatten the list, while Listing 5.7 uses list.append.

```python
def append_flatten_lists(
    the_lists: List[List[str]]) -> List[str]:
    """
    Flatten a list of lists via nested append
    """

    result: List[str] = []
    for _list in the_lists:
        for val in _list:
            result.append(val)
    return result
```

```
for sub_list in the_lists:
    for val in sub_list:
        result.append(val)

[val for sub_list in the_lists for val in sub_list]
```


Figure 5.1: Nested list comprehension explainer

Listing 5.7: Append flatten lists

Listing 5.8 uses a brain-bending nested list comprehension.

```python
def comprehension_flatten_lists(
    the_lists: List[List[str]]) -> List[str]:
    """
    Flatten a list of lists via nested list comprehension
    """
    return [val for _list in the_lists for val in _list]
```

Listing 5.8: Comprehension flatten lists

To better understand how Listing 5.8 works, and to better understand nested list comprehensions in general, compare Listing 5.8 to Listing 5.7. If you pretend the white space and semicolons aren't there, a nested for loop looks just like a nested list comprehension, except the `val` that is added to the list occurs at the beginning in a comprehension. See Figure 5.1 for a visual explanation.

See Table 5.2 and Figures 5.4 and 5.5 for execution times of list flattening methods. Without profiling, it would have been impossible to predict that `add_flatten_lists` is the fastest method. From the standpoint of a Python programmer that has not read the C-level source code for these list operations, there is no logical reason why `add_flatten_lists` should outperform the other methods. Nonetheless, it is obvious from the profiles that it is the best. We should keep that fact in the back of our minds while we program.

Given these perplexing results, it is worthwhile to investigate how

list objects work. See Listing 5.9 for sizing tables for lists of various
lengths.

```python
import sys

for i in range(100):
    _list = [(j+0.1)**2 for j in range(i)]
    _list_size = sys.getsizeof(_list)
    print(f'{len(_list):<8} values {_list_size:>12} bytes')

# Returns ...
# 0          values          72 bytes
# 1          values         104 bytes
# 2          values         104 bytes
# 3          values         104 bytes
# 4          values         104 bytes
# 5          values         136 bytes
# 6          values         136 bytes
# 7          values         136 bytes
# 8          values         136 bytes
# 9          values         200 bytes
# 10         values         200 bytes
# 11         values         200 bytes
# 12         values         200 bytes
# 13         values         200 bytes
# ...

from utils.profiler import ExponentialRange
exp_range = ExponentialRange(0, 7, 1/4)

for i in exp_range.iterator():
    _list = [(j+0.1)**2 for j in range(i)]
    _list_size = sys.getsizeof(_list)
    print(f'{len(_list):<8} values {_list_size:>12} bytes')

# Returns ...
# 1          values         104 bytes
# 3          values         104 bytes
# 5          values         136 bytes
# 10         values         200 bytes
# 17         values         272 bytes
# 31         values         352 bytes
```

```
# 56          values           536 bytes
# 100         values           920 bytes
# 177         values          1680 bytes
# 316         values          2904 bytes
# 562         values          4856 bytes
# 1000        values          9032 bytes
# ...
```

Listing 5.9: List sizing breakpoints

From Listing 5.9, we can see that the number of bytes in a list object is not exactly proportional to the number of elements in it. Python allocates memory to lists based on the number of elements in a bracketed fashion. For example, the size in bytes of a 1-element list is the same as that of a 4-element list. The same goes for lengths 5 through 8, 9 through 16, 17 through 25, and so on.

It is not important to understand exactly how this bracketing works, and it is not totally necessary to understand how memory allocation works with Python lists. It is only important to understand that Python does not give us fine-grained control over memory allocation, so we must deal with whatever optimizations are or are not present. Profiling is important because different distributions of Python might or might not contain certain optimizations. Use this book as a guide, but also feel free to test your own Python distribution to see if it matches this behavior. Either way, you will reveal the fastest way to do common tasks like flattening lists.

f	n	t (ms)	n/t
slow_add_flatten_lists	1E+04	8.8E+02	1.1E+01
add_flatten_lists	1E+07	4.3E+02	2.3E+04
extend_flatten_lists	1E+07	6.6E+02	1.5E+04
append_flatten_lists	1E+07	4.0E+03	2.5E+03
comprehension_flatten_lists	1E+07	1.5E+03	6.6E+03

Table 5.2: List flattening performance

5.3 Declaring Dictionaries

Dictionaries behave similarly to lists in the sense that they have sizing brackets, but the brackets are wider. This makes sense given what we know about hash tables. Functional hash tables need to have excess space in order to work efficiently.

```python
import sys

from utils.profiler import ExponentialRange
exp_range = ExponentialRange(0, 7, 1/8)

for i in exp_range.iterator():
    _dict = {j: j**2 for j in range(i)}
    _dict_size = sys.getsizeof(_dict)
    print(f'{len(_dict):<8} keys {_dict_size:>12} bytes')

# Returns ...
# 1          keys              248 bytes
# 2          keys              248 bytes
# 3          keys              248 bytes
# 4          keys              248 bytes
# 5          keys              248 bytes
# 7          keys              376 bytes
# 10         keys              376 bytes
# 13         keys              656 bytes
# 17         keys              656 bytes
# 23         keys             1192 bytes
# 31         keys             1192 bytes
# 42         keys             1192 bytes
# 56         keys             2288 bytes
# 74         keys             2288 bytes
# 100        keys             4712 bytes
# ...
```

Listing 5.10: Dictionary sizing breakpoints

We will go through the same exercises we did with lists on dictionaries in order to figure out the fastest generic method of declaring them. To test the fastest way to declare a dictionary, we will take a list of random words and create a dictionary of each unique word pointing to itself.

See Listing 5.11 for a few methods of declaring dictionaries. These results and functions do not need a lot of explanation. The dictionary comprehension is fastest, followed by the loop, followed by the generator, and ending with the list. This is exactly in-line with our expectations according to the simplicity of the code itself.

```python
def loop_build_dict(words: List[str]) -> Dict[str, str]:
    """
    Build a dictionary by looping through each element of
    the list and declaring it as the key-value pair
    """
    result = dict()
    for word in words:
        result[word] = word
    return result

def list_build_dict(
    words: List[str]) -> Dict[str, str]:
    """
    Build a dictionary by passing a list of tuples to the
    dict constructor
    """
    return dict([(w, w) for w in words])

def generator_build_dict(
    words: List[str]) -> Dict[str, str]:
    """
    Build a dictionary by passing a generator of tuples to
    the dict constructor
    """
    return dict(((w, w) for w in words))

def comprehension_build_dict(
    words: List[str]) -> Dict[str, str]:
    """
    Build a dictionary using a dict comprehension
    """
    return {w: w for w in words}
```

Listing 5.11: Declaring dictionaries

f	n	t (ms)	n/t
loop_build_dict	1E+07	2.3E+03	4.3E+03
list_build_dict	1E+07	3.5E+03	2.8E+03
generator_build_dict	1E+07	2.7E+03	3.7E+03
comprehension_build_dict	1E+07	2.2E+03	4.6E+03

Table 5.3: Declaring dictionaries

5.4   Conclusion

This chapter could easily get very dry if it went on much longer. We affirmed some obvious things, then discovered one interesting thing, that the `+=` operator sometimes provides the fastest interface to list construction. We will close out the book with miscellaneous tips on various topics in Python programming. The following chapter is one that I hope will expand as more novel examples are shared by readers online.

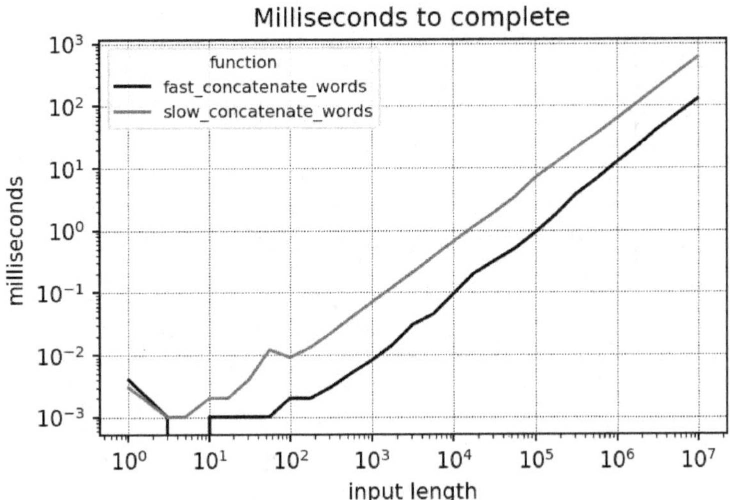

Figure 5.2: String concatenation execution time

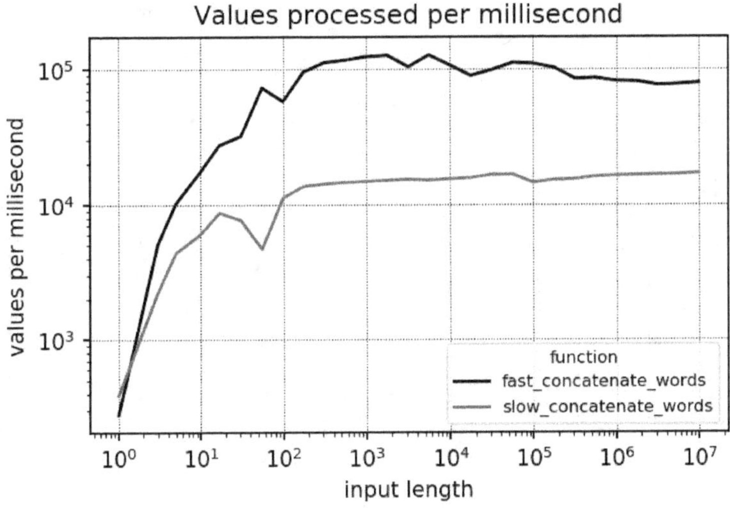

Figure 5.3: String concatenation efficiency

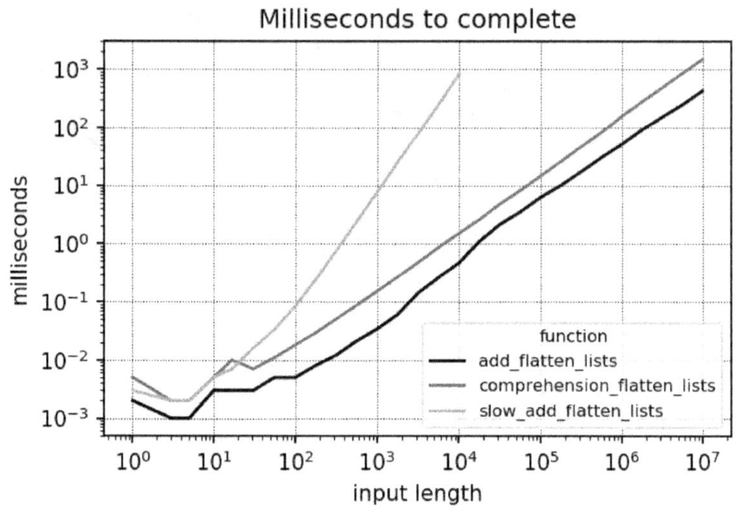

Figure 5.4: List flattening execution time

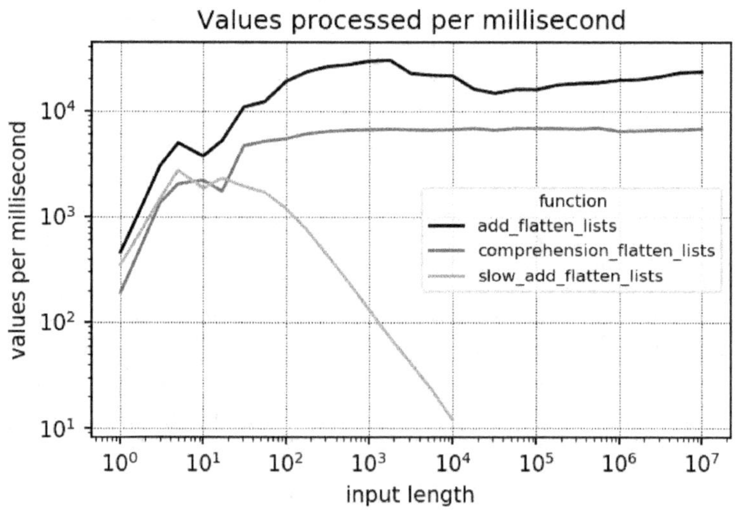

Figure 5.5: List flattening efficiency

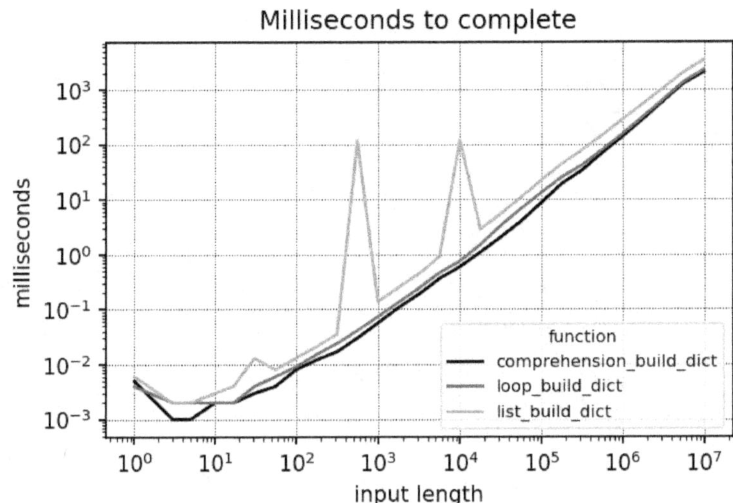

Figure 5.6: Declaring dictionaries execution time

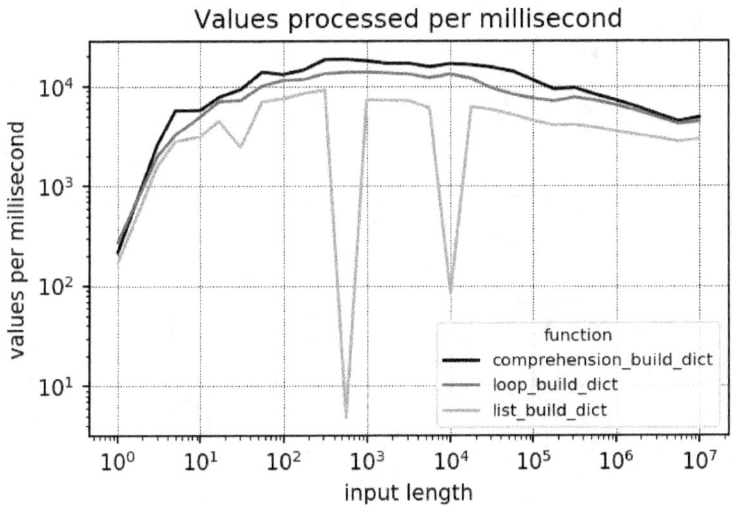

Figure 5.7: Declaring dictionaries efficiency

Chapter 6

Miscellaneous Topics

Everything you need to know to write fast Python code is contained in the first five chapters of this book. In those chapters, we have covered computational efficiency, memory efficiency, vectorization, compilation, multi-threading and data structures.

Using very simple examples, we have elucidated all of the fundamentals of writing fast code in an interpreted language. Any further explanation would be redundant.

This chapter will cover miscellaneous topics in code optimization that could not find a place elsewhere in the book. We will forgo lengthy examples and profiles in some cases in favor of general guidance.

6.1   SQL and SQL Queries

For those entirely unfamiliar with SQL and common design patterns for working with SQL-based data stores, consider the following. SQL-based data stores like MySQL, MariaDB, SQLite3, and PostgreSQL typically run in a client-server model, where the *SQL server* runs in the background while the client makes queries to the server to create, read, update, and delete data. In this model, the client is your Python code. The data transfer occurs using the SQL, which stands for *structured query language*.

Python has a number of useful libraries for working with SQL-based data stores, often in ways that do not require the programmer write any SQL code. These libraries are generally called *object relational models* or ORMs, because they map Python objects to relational data structures. Popular ORMs include Django and SQLAlchemy.

If you currently or have every worked with such technologies, you likely know all of this already. What is not widely appreciated, however, is where and how bottlenecks occur in ORMs. The most common problems I see with projects using ORMs are poorly structured data models and poorly structured queries. This section will address some of those problems using some sample code with the Django ORM.

Note that the sample code will not run as-is, because it is not appropriately structured within a Django project. It is written here for sake of exposition. Readers that are specifically interested in Django should check out the sample projects in their documentation.

6.1.1 Sample Data Structure

For sake of discussion, consider the following data structure in Django.

```python
from django.db import models

class Author(models.Model):
    name = models.CharField(max_length=254, unique=True)

class Book(models.Model):
    author = models.ForeignKey(
        Author,
        on_delete=models.CASCADE
    )
    title = models.CharField(max_length=254, db_index=True)
    subtitle = models.CharField(max_length=254)
```

Listing 6.1: Sample data structure in Django

This data structure describes a simple relationship between two simple objects, which correspond to two SQL tables. The database has a table of authors that are uniquely identified by their name, and a table of books which much reference an author. The book objects also contain information about their title and subtitle. Creating some records in the database might look like the following.

When you `migrate` this object into the database, Django will generate and run the following SQL code.

```
CREATE TABLE "bookstore_author" (
    "id" integer NOT NULL PRIMARY KEY AUTOINCREMENT,
    "name" varchar(254) NOT NULL UNIQUE
); args=None

CREATE TABLE "bookstore_book" (
    "id" integer NOT NULL PRIMARY KEY AUTOINCREMENT,
    "title" varchar(254) NOT NULL,
    "subtitle" varchar(254) NOT NULL,
    "author_id" integer NOT NULL REFERENCES
    "bookstore_author" ("id") DEFERRABLE INITIALLY DEFERRED
); args=None

CREATE INDEX "bookstore_book_title_40d52b28" ON
    "bookstore_book" ("title"); args=()

CREATE INDEX "bookstore_book_author_id_c8c6315b" ON
    "bookstore_book" ("author_id"); args=()
```

Listing 6.2: Creating the SQL tables in Django

This SQL code creates the tables with all the accouterments we specified. If we want to create some objects in the database, we might do the following.

```
from bookstore.models import Author, Book

some_author = Author(name='Chris Conlan')
some_author.save()

some_book = Book(
    author=some_author,
    title='Fast Python',
    subtitle='Master the basics'
)
some_book.save()
```

Listing 6.3: Creating some sample objects in Django

This would cause the following SQL code to run.

```
INSERT INTO "bookstore_author"
    ("name") VALUES (
        'Chris Conlan'
); args=['Chris Conlan']

INSERT INTO "bookstore_book"
    ("author_id", "title", "subtitle") VALUES (
        1,
        'Fast Python',
        'Master the basics'
); args=[1, 'Fast Python', 'Master the basics']
```

Listing 6.4: Create sample objects in SQL

Now, imagine this database belongs to Amazon, so it has millions of books in it. Also, imagine I am an extremely prolific writer and I have hundreds of books in this database. If I wanted to query all of the books I have written, I would do something like the following.

```
my_books = Book.objects.filter(author__name='Chris Conlan')
```

Listing 6.5: Querying my books in Django

Listing 6.5 generates and executes the following SQL code.

```
SELECT
    "bookstore_book"."id",
    "bookstore_book"."author_id",
    "bookstore_book"."title",
    "bookstore_book"."subtitle" FROM

    "bookstore_book" INNER JOIN "bookstore_author" ON (
        "bookstore_book"."author_id" =
        "bookstore_author"."id"
) WHERE "bookstore_author"."name" = 'Chris Conlan'
    LIMIT 21;

args=('Chris Conlan',)
```

Listing 6.6: Querying my books in SQL

Now, I can manipulate my data in Python using the following.

```python
for book in my_books:
    print(f'{book.title} by {book.author.name}')
```

Listing 6.7: Manipulating the data in Python

Even if you have not read or written SQL before, it is not too difficult to see the similarities between the Python code and the auto-generated SQL code. Using this sample data structure, we will discuss the two most important ways to speed up your ORM code.

6.1.2 Optimizing Queries

Databases are a very old and mature technology. They are highly optimized internally, and they provide numerous facilities for optimizing them towards your specific use case. One such facility, called *indexes*, allow us to reduce the computational complexity of queries from within the database itself.

Imagine, again, that our bookstore database contains millions of books, and you wanted to get this book out of the database. In Django, you might do something like the following.

```python
# This is O(log(n)) because title is an indexed field
this_book = Book.objects.get(
    title='Fast Python'
)


# This is O(n) because subtitle is not indexed
also_this_book = Book.objects.get(
    subtitle='Master the basics'
)
```

Listing 6.8: Querying indexed fields

Remember from our earlier data model that we pass db_index=True to the **name** field of Book. Recall also how the SQL statement   CREATE INDEX "bookstore_book_title_40d52b28" ON "bookstore_book" ("title"); ran as a result. Indexing a field creates an external index table in the database that is responsible for managing and maintaining the sort order of that field within the table. In the database itself, the data is ordered roughly by the insertion order of the objects. The index attribute allows queries on that field to utilize a binary search to locate their position, resulting in $\mathcal{O}(\log(n))$ lookup time for a table with n rows. The equivalent lookup time for a non-indexed field is $\mathcal{O}(n)$, because the database itself has no advance knowledge of the sort order of an unindexed attribute.

There is some cost, however, to indexing a field. Because the sort order index has to be updated and maintained continuously, the insertion time of indexed fields is $\mathcal{O}(\log(n))$. We know this because we know that binary trees allow for insertion time of $\mathcal{O}(\log(n))$ on already-sorted lists of values. As a result, the insertion time for an object in a database table with m indexed fields is $\mathcal{O}(m \log(n))$, resulting from the need to update m binary trees each time an insertion is performed. This is the reason it is almost never helpful to index every single field of a database table.

Although the math regarding computational complexity is less simple, lookups on indexed fields are significantly faster for queries on both single elements and multiple elements.

It is worth noting that databases utilize the general theory around binary tree searches for indexed fields, but they also go above and beyond that on a platform-specific basis. Such optimization are often so significant that lookups on indexed fields can be regarded as $O(1)$ for tables with fewer than 100,000 elements.

Look back to Listing 6.2 and note how the `Author.name` field was initialized in SQL using the command `"name" varchar(254) NOT NULL UNIQUE`. It is worth noting that the uniqueness constraint in SQL also results in the construction of an index table. In other words, passing both `unique=True` and `db_index=True` to a Django field is redundant. The `unique=True` parameter implies `db_index=True`. The only difference between these two arguments is that database indexes are not required to be unique, whereas unique fields are. Under this data structure, SQL will throw an error if we attempt to insert two authors with the same name into the database.

This subsection detailed how optimizing the performance of the database itself around your specific use case can create speed advantages. The next subsection will talk about how reducing the number of queries you make to the database can speed up your Python code.

6.1.3 Minimizing Queries

Recall that Python libraries interface with SQL-based data stores via a client-server model. Let us discuss exactly how that happens. For example, the following occurs when you query a book by title as in Listing 6.8.

1. The user calls `Book.objects.get(title='...')`.
2. Django translates the call into a SQL query as a string.
3. Django sends the SQL query string to the SQL server.
4. The SQL server parses the string into a query it can run against the data.
5. The SQL server runs the query and determines which objects satisfy the query conditions.
6. The SQL server serializes the relevant data to a SQL string.
7. The SQL server sends that string back to Django through the open connection.
8. Django parses the SQL string into a Python object according to its corresponding class definition.

One query to a SQL server involves one request-response cycle where each side much parse a SQL string, perform an internal operation, and construct a SQL string. However complicated this sounds, it is perfectly normal, and largely resembles the way we make requests to websites using HTTP and HTML. It is, however, computationally expensive. Both sides of the transaction are fast, mature, and optimized, but we still want to absolutely minimize the number of queries we make to the SQL server in order to maximize speed.

When I work on Django projects, I practice this by logging the SQL statements to a file. Then, I simply count the number of **SELECT** statements that are made. If I accomplish a given task with fewer **SELECT** statements in my log files, I have sped up my code. This section will present some common design patterns for minimizing the number of queries made to the server.

As an aside, I have seen projects where developers are entirely ignorant to this concept. They typically result in webpages that require 20,000+ queries and take about 20 seconds to load. In those cases, I have been able to use the following concepts to reduce the number of queries to around 4 or 5 and speed up page loads by 100-fold.

```python
def slow_get_author_ids(names: List[str]) -> List[int]:
    """
    Given a list of author names, return a list of their
    database ids (primary key values). This is O(n) because
    it performs n SQL queries
    """
    author_ids = list()
    for name in names:
        # This results in a single query
        author = Author.objects.get(name=name)
        author_ids.append(author.id)
    return author_ids
```

Listing 6.9: Slow get author IDs

Say we have a list of authors we got from some external source, and
we want to know all of the database IDs. The list of author names
might look like this **names = ['Chris Conlan', 'Edgar Allen
Poe', ...]**. Listing 6.9 shows how to do this with n queries, while
Listing 6.10 shows how to do this with 1 query.

```python
def fast_get_author_ids(names: List[str]) -> List[int]:
    """
    Given a list of author names, return a list of their
    database ids (primary key values). This is O(1) because
    it performs 1 SQL query
    """
    author_ids = Author.objects\
        .filter(name__in=names)\
        .values_list('id', flat=True)
    return list(author_ids)
```

Listing 6.10: Fast get author IDs

Listing 6.10 is nearly n times faster than Listing 6.9 for large lists,
because it makes n times fewer network requests.

6.1.4   Eliminating Hidden Queries

Django is really easy to use, but that ease-of-use can be your enemy
if you are not aware of how Django manages database queries. For
example, if you query a row in the books table, Django will send a
SQL **SELECT** statement for that row in the books table. What about

the author of the book? The attribute `Book.author` represents an `Author` object whose information is stored in a row in the authors table. In other words, just because you queried a book, it does not mean you queried the corresponding author. If you haven't queried the corresponding author, Django will make the query for you and store the result in `book.author` for future use. This is useful, but it can introduce hidden queries. See Listing 6.11 for an example.

```python
# 1 SELECT query on the book table
some_book = Book.objects.get(title='Fast Python')

# No queries
print(some_book.title)

# No queries
print(some_book.author_id)

# 1 SELECT query on the author table
print(some_book.author.id)

# No queries, because author is now cached
print(some_book.author.name)

###

# 1 JOIN query on books and authors
another_book = Book.objects\
    .filter(title='Faster Python')\
    .select_related('author')\
    .get()

# No queries for any of these
print(another_book.title)
print(another_book.author_id)
print(another_book.author.id)
print(another_book.author.name)
```

Listing 6.11: How and when Django issues queries

We see that the first interaction with `some_book` results in two queries, but the second interaction with `another_book` results in one query. Notice how `author_id` is an attribute on the books table that does not require a query, but `author.id` is not an attribute on the books table and thus requires a query. The `book.author_id` attribute represents an integer in the books table pointing to an author row in the author table, but `book.author.id` refers to the primary key of the author row as recorded in the author table. Thus, to access the data in `Book.author`, Django needs to issue a **SELECT** statement to the author table if it has not retrieved that information in advance.

This hidden query complexity becomes significant when we are dealing with multiples books. See Listings 6.12 and 6.13 for alternative ways to collect all books according to their author's name.

```python
def slow_get_books_by_author() -> Dict[str, List[Book]]:
    """
    Organize all books in the database into a dictionary
    where the books are stored in a list identified by their
    author's name. This requires n+1 queries for n rows
    in the books table.
    """

    # This queries just the books table
    books = Book.objects.all()
    books_by_author = dict()
    for book in books:
        # This results in a query on the author table
        name = book.author.name
        if not name in books_by_author:
            books_by_author[name] = list()
        books_by_author[name].append(book)
    return books_by_author
```

Listing 6.12: Slow get books by author

The `.select_related` statement allows us to issue **JOIN** requests to SQL telling it to pull in the author data along with the books data. As a result, Django does not have to issue **SELECT** statements to the author table each time a book's author's information is requested.

```python
def fast_get_books_by_author() -> Dict[str, List[Book]]:
    """
    Organize all books in the database into a dictionary
    where the books are stored in a list identified by their
    author's name. This requires 1 JOIN query for n rows
    in the books table.
```

```python
    """
    # This queries books and authors tables simultaneously
    books = Book.objects.all().select_related('author')
    books_by_author = dict()
    for book in books:
        # This does not require a query
        name = book.author.name
        if not name in books_by_author:
            books_by_author[name] = list()
        books_by_author[name].append(book)
    return books_by_author
```

Listing 6.13: Fast get books by author

Listing 6.13 will run approximately n times faster than Listing 6.12 for n total rows in the database. Concepts like these are extremely important for the scalability of SQL-based applications, most notably web applications. Could you imagine using Facebook or Twitter if every time the user count doubled, the page loads took twice as long?

SQL has been around for a long time. Some old-school SQL advocates encourage moving away from ORMs altogether, because they supposedly encourage the generation of this type of bad SQL code. I do not agree with this sentiment. As long as ORM users understand how SQL works, they can be used effectively.

6.2 Pandas and Loops

In my most recent book, *Algorithmic Trading with Python*, I wrangled with **pandas** a lot. There some quirky speed tricks I would like to share here.

6.2.1 Looping through Data Frames

There are a lot of ways to loop through `pd.DataFrame` objects. The default recommendation I would give to anyone working with data frames is to always use the `pd.DataFrame.itertuples()` function, because it is the fastest pure-Pandas solution. The equation changes a little bit when we want to work with complex data frames, like those with dynamic column names or hierarchical column indexes.

For these examples, we will attempt to loop through a data frame as quickly as possible and store the value of the last column of each row in-memory, all while assuming we do not know the name of the last column. This appropriately simulates a lot of common but complex scenarios where the column names are dynamic.

```python
def index_loop_df(df: pd.DataFrame):
    """
    Use the pandas index to look up the row at each step.
    pandas indexes are dict-like, so the lookup in O(1).
    """
    last_column = df.columns.values[-1]
    for i in df.index:
        row: pd.Series = df.loc[i]
        val = row[last_column]
```

Listing 6.14: Index loop through data frame

Listings 6.14 and 6.15 show how to access the row of a data frame by using the .loc and .iloc attributes. The .loc attribute allows you to access the row by the value of the index. Indexes can be anything, including integers, dates, and strings, as we discussed earlier. The .iloc attribute allows you to access rows according to their range-based position. For example, df.iloc[5] accesses the sixth row, as though df were a normal Python list.

The .index is dict-like in Pandas, so computational complexity is not an issue here. Given that index lookups are typically a little faster than hash table lookups, we should expect Listing 6.15 to be a little faster than Listing 6.14.

```python
def iloc_loop_df(df: pd.DataFrame):
    """
    Use the a range-based index to look up the row at each
    step, side-stepping the index. This should skip a
    hashing operation and be faster than the index lookup.
    """
    last_column = df.columns.values[-1]
    for i in range(df.shape[0]):
        row: pd.Series = df.iloc[i]
        val = row[last_column]
```

Listing 6.15: iloc loop through data frame

Listing 6.16 uses the recommended way of looping through a Pandas data frame, `.iterrows()`. This function generates an iterator that returns both the index and the row of each row of the data frame as a `pd.Series` object. This is the approach recommended by the Pandas documentation because it preserves the feature-rich API of `pd.Series` objects. For example, because the row is a series, you can call things like `row.sum()` and `row.value_counts()`.

```python
def iterrows_loop_df(df: pd.DataFrame):
    """
    Iterrows is the vanilla and recommended solution for
    looping through data frames
    """

    last_column = df.columns.values[-1]
    for i, row in df.iterrows():
        # row is a pd.Series
        val = row[last_column]
```

Listing 6.16: Iterrows loop through data frame

Listing 6.17 uses `.itertuples()` to loop through the data frame. This is the method I prefer, because I rarely end up needing to use features of `pd.Series` when in the middle of a loop. Typically, when your use-case has necessitated a loop, you have stepped out of the bounds of what Pandas explicitly supports. In other words, you are consciously circumventing the API. In these situations, you rarely need access to the features of `pd.Series` objects.

This method has been up to three times faster for me in the past, but it is only slightly faster in our profiles. The `row` in this scenario is an object similar to a `collections.namedtuple`, which allows element-wise access via `row.XYZ` or `row[i]`. Since we assume we do not know the column name in advance, we make a mapping of each column name to each range-based index. Even with the added overhead of dictionary lookups, this loop is still faster than the previous one.

```python
def itertuples_loop_df(df: pd.DataFrame):
    """
    .itertuples doesn't allow named-based indexing of
    closures, but it does allow range-based indexing, so
    we map each column to its range-based position
    beforehand.
    """
```

```python
    """
    last_column = df.columns.values[-1]

    # Use i+1 because row[0] is the index
    col_index_by_name = {
        col: i+1 for i, col in enumerate(df.columns.values)
    }

    for row in df.itertuples():
        # Row is type pd.core.frame.Pandas,
        # which appears to be a private object
        # similar to a collections.namedtuple
        val = row[col_index_by_name[last_column]]
```

Listing 6.17: Itertuples loop through data frame

The final method involves converting the Pandas data frame to a
numpy array using `.values` attribute. This attribute is available
on all **pd.Dataframe** and **pd.Series** objects, and it can be useful
in scenarios like these. This loop blows all of the others out of the
water in terms of speed, being nearly 100 times faster, but it is not
memory-friendly. This requires that a copy of the data frame be
made and temporarily stored as the iterator variable in order to
work. Additionally, it risks losing support for any data types that
are not **numpy** compatible.

```python
def values_loop_df(df: pd.DataFrame):
    """
    .values converts the data frame to a numpy array before
    looping, which is fast but no memory-friendly
    """
    last_column = df.columns.values[-1]
    col_index_by_name = {
        col: i for i, col in enumerate(df.columns.values)
    }
    for row in df.values:
        val = row[col_index_by_name[last_column]]
```

Listing 6.18: Values loop through data frame

See the table below for execution time on the above loops. We will
forgo profile charts in this section since all of the algorithms are
$\mathcal{O}(n)$.

f	n	t (ms)	n/t
`index_loop_df`	1E+05	9.5E+03	1.1E+01
`iloc_loop_df`	1E+05	8.1E+03	1.2E+01
`iterrows_loop_df`	1E+05	5.1E+03	2.0E+01
`itertuples_loop_df`	1E+05	4.1E+03	2.4E+01
`values_loop_df`	1E+05	3.2E+01	3.2E+03

Table 6.1: Pandas loops

6.3 Conclusion

As we wrap up our discussion of computational complexity and code profiling, keep the following in mind.

- It is essential to appreciate the foundations of computer science to write fast code.
- Computational complexity provides guidance but not a solution to writing fast code.
- Profiling provides us measurements but not advice for writing fast code.
- Profiles can surprise you, so test many potential solutions.
- Appreciate both the capabilities and limits of computers.

Writing this book has been very enjoyable and rewarding. At my company, I am a stickler about speed. I try to educate my employees on how to write fast code the first time, and I use the principles of computational complexity to guide important business decisions on behalf of my clients. Then, other times, I find myself profiling code just to win arguments.

I hope that this little book is well-received by novices and veterans for the lesser-known facts it highlights, and I hope to continue to interact with readers through GitHub and Reddit to add interesting examples and content to it.

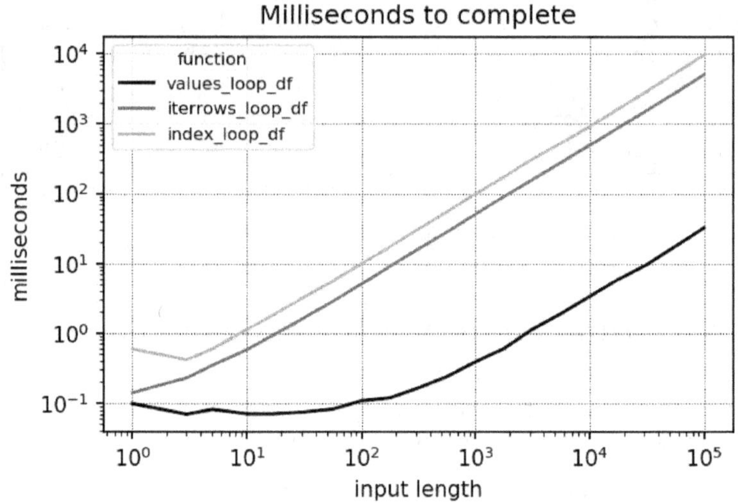

Figure 6.1: Dataframe loop efficiency

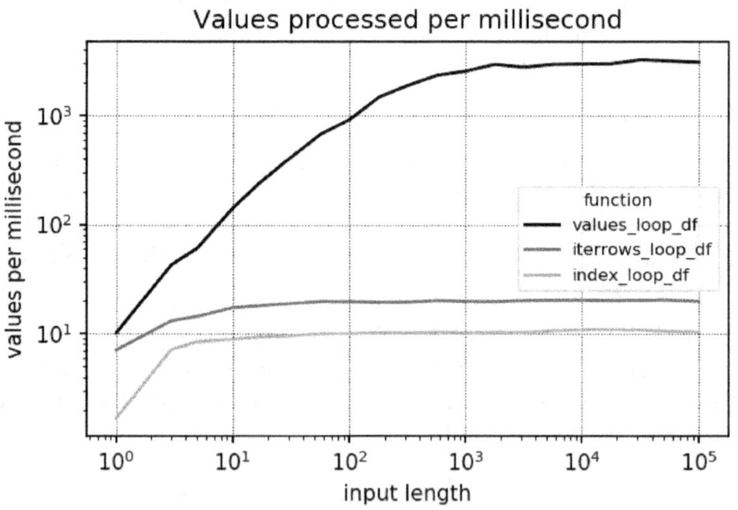

Figure 6.2: Dataframe loop execution time